Collected Poems

by Philip Larkin

poetry
The North Ship
XX Poems
The Fantasy Poets No. 21
The Less Deceived
(*The Marvell Press*)
The Whitsun Weddings
High Windows

The Oxford Book of Twentieth-Century English Verse (Ed.)

fiction
Jill
A Girl in Winter

non-fiction
All What Jazz: A Record Diary 1961–71
Required Writing: Miscellaneous Pieces 1955–82

Philip Larkin

Collected Poems

EDITED

WITH AN INTRODUCTION BY

ANTHONY THWAITE

WITHDRAWN

FARRAR · STRAUS · GIROUX

and

THE MARVELL PRESS

Contents

[xi]

[xii]

Acknowledgements

I must acknowledge the help, co-operation and advice of the following: my fellow trustees and literary executors, Monica Jones, Andrew Motion and Terence Wheldon; Kingsley Amis; B. C. Bloomfield; Maeve Brennan; Alan Brownjohn; Judy Egerton; Alistair Elliot; Barbara Everett; George Hartley; Anthony Hedges; Hazel Holt; Noel Hughes; Mark Le Fanu; David Long; Christopher McCall; George MacBeth; Charles Madge; Michael Millgate; Brenda Moon; Blake Morrison; Peter Porter; Alan Ross; J. B. Sutton; A. T. Tolley; the staff of the Brynmor Jones Library, University of Hull; the staff of the Department of Manuscripts, British Library; the staff of the Modern MSS and John Johnson Reading Room, Bodleian Library, Oxford; and my wife, Ann Thwaite.

Acknowledgments

Introduction

This edition aims to include, first, the poems completed by Philip Larkin between 1946 and the end of his life, together with a few unfinished poems which Larkin preserved in typescript; and, second, a substantial selection of his earlier poems, from 1938 until the end of 1945. In the first section, sixty-one poems appear in print here for the first time; in the second, of the earlier poems, twenty-two. In each section, all the poems are arranged in chronological order of completion, determined whenever possible by Larkin's precise dating of manuscript or typescript: when such dates are lacking, I have had to rely on other evidence, usually – in the case of published poems – on the date of publication.

It is clear from the first of Larkin's extant manuscript note-books (dated 5 October 1944–10 March 1950, and given by him to the British Library in 1965) that the earliest poems which strike his characteristic note and carry his own voice were written in 1946. It seemed to make sense to begin the main body of this collected volume with the first poem of his maturity which he chose to preserve ('Going', see p.3), written early that year, and then to follow this with the subsequent poems; and to relegate the earlier poems (1938–45) to a separate section. This means that the contents of *The North Ship*, published in July 1945, are among those labelled 'Early Poems' (with the exception of one poem, 'Waiting for breakfast', written in December 1947, and added by Larkin to the 1966 edition of that book).

Larkin's reputation as a poet did not, in fact, begin with *The North Ship*, which on its first appearance was hardly noticed. It was with the publication of *The Less Deceived*, late in 1955 when he was thirty-three, that he began to be recognized. By the time he died thirty years later, he had become one of the best-known poets in the English-speaking world, and one of the best loved. His reputation was based on a small body of work; and during his lifetime the general impression of his actual output of poems was that it was sparse – an impression Larkin did nothing to dispel. There were long gaps between the publication of his three mature books: *The Less Deceived* was followed in 1964 by *The Whitsun Weddings*, and finally, in 1974, by *High Windows*. After *High Windows*, in the remaining eleven years of his life, Larkin made public only eight poems; and this is to count such slight, occasional or fugitive pieces as the celebratory stanza for the opening of the new university library in Hull, the eightieth-birthday tribute to Sir Brynmor Jones, the sixty-fifth birthday poem for Charles Causley, and the quatrain commissioned for the 1977 Jubilee by the Trustees of Queen Square garden and inscribed on a memorial stone there in 1978.

It may come as a surprise that the quantity of Larkin's uncollected and unpublished poetry should be so large. His youthful copiousness is documented. In his essay 'Not the Place's Fault' (1959), remembering his Coventry boyhood up until his going up to Oxford at the age of eighteen, he commented: 'I wrote ceaselessly . . . : now verse, which I sewed up into little books, now prose, a thousand words a night after homework . . .' Four of these typed 'little books' survive, from September 1939, March 1940, June 1940, and August 1940, together with three later typed booklets from April 1941 and January and July 1942, when he was at Oxford. A few of these poems were published, in the school magazine (*The Coventrian*) or in Oxford magazines and anthologies: Larkin kept an exercise book in which he pasted printed copies of seventeen of them, beginning with 'Winter Nocturne' (p.225) and ending with 'Portrait' (p.309). No working notebooks or drafts seem to survive of any poems written between 1938 and the autumn of 1944: the order followed in the present edition is either that of publication date, or, with the unpublished poems from the 'little books', I have usually had to rely on the overall dates typed on their title pages by Larkin, and on the dates and remarks he occasionally attached to them.

Thus it seems impossible to give anything like firm dates to many of the poems in *The North Ship*, until the first dated entry ('If grief could burn out', 5 October 1944, see p.298) in the earliest surviving manuscript notebook. But I feel that all the poems from 'All catches alight' (p.272) to 'Pour away that youth' (p.297) must have been written between the spring of 1943 and September 1944, and mainly from the autumn of 1943.

The British Library's manuscript notebook is the first of eight such folio notebooks, kept by Larkin between October 1944 and November 1980. It was Larkin's usual practice, certainly from 1946 onwards, to move from his pencil-written notebook drafts to a typed draft at a late stage of a poem's composition, and then to make small changes by hand on the typescript. He also kept a folder of neat final typescripts, labelled 'Unpublished Poems 1948– '. He tended to date his notebook drafts as they progressed, but not, for the most part, his typescripts. However, his notebook dating was so meticulous, and was usually carried so close to a poem's completion, that in most cases one can establish a specific day for both the beginning and the end of a poem.

The notebooks show that, from 1949 on, Larkin was an intensive worker at his drafts. The beginning of a poem and its completion often lay far apart. For example, his first attempt at 'Love Songs in Age' was made in July 1953, but it was then dropped and not taken up again until December 1956, being completed on 1 January 1957. 'Take One Home for the Kiddies' was begun in April 1954, set aside, and then brought to completion in August 1960. 'Church Going', begun on 24 April 1954, went through twenty-one pages of drafts, was 'abandoned 24.5.54', and then resumed and completed in July of that year. 'The Whitsun Weddings', begun in May 1957 with its first stanza complete, was then dropped, resumed in July 1958, reworked for twenty-three pages until 6 September, picked up again on 19 September and completed after eight further pages of drafts on 18 October.

Philip Larkin always maintained that, after his fertile adolescence, he was a meagre poet. True, the evidence of the notebooks shows what appear to be completely blank periods: most of 1947 and 1948, the whole of 1952, much of 1957–8, and – with sporadic exceptions – after 1975. But the notebooks also show something rather different. He had some extremely prolific periods: from October 1944 to November 1946; during part of his time in Belfast, particularly in 1950–1 and in 1953–4; in Hull between 1960 and 1962, and again between 1971 and 1973.

It is true that I have found little (only seven further poems) to add to the small known tally subsequent to the publication of *High Windows* in 1974. In June of that year Larkin moved from his 'high windows' flat to the house in Hull which was his home until his death. In his usual sardonic and sometimes lugubrious way, he made much of the horrors of this. It does not, however, seem fanciful to me to connect this move – 'audacious, purifying, elemental', but also traumatic – with the coming to a virtual standstill of his poems. The responsibility of running a university library which, when he took it over in 1955, was 'a nice little Shetland pony', but which under his guidance had grown into 'a frightful Grand National winner', seems to have been a factor too, draining away much energy. There was Larkin's increasing fame as a poet, something which depressed and even frightened him. He accepted and enjoyed some of the honour sometimes, but found it an inhibiting burden too. And there gradually began those ills of age that he so much dreaded, premonitions as they were of 'the only end of age'.

To have included all of Larkin's available surviving 1938–45 poems would, I think, have been a mistake. As I said at the beginning, I have made a substantial selection. All the published but uncollected poems are here and, of course, the whole of *The North Ship*. The earliest poems are what Larkin, in the preface to the 1939 'little book', called 'pseudo-Keats babble'. A little later there is the brief influence of T. S. Eliot:

The dull whole of the drawing room
Is crucified with crystal nails,
Dresden shepherdesses smirk
As Stanley practises his scales.

From the beginning of 1940, a few months after his seventeenth birthday, the stamp of W. H. Auden is plain. In the foreword to a typed booklet with the title *chosen poems 1941*, dated April of that year, Larkin wrote:

'As for their literary interest, I think that almost any single line by Auden would be worth more than the whole lot put together. The course of ossification, in fact, is concurrent with the gradually increasing traces of the Auden manner (and is possibly the cause of it) until towards the end the poems are to be judged solely by comparison with the Auden of "Look, Stranger!" Certainly they are not very similar, but Auden's ease and vividness were the qualities I most wished to gain.'

These poems, beginning here with 'Nothing significant was really said' (p.235), and including 'Ultimatum', first published in the *Listener* in November 1940 (p.243), are indeed consummately Audenesque. This domination seems to last about three years, during most of Larkin's time at Oxford. It is then abruptly replaced by that of Yeats, mediated to some extent by Vernon Watkins and Watkins's own hieratic Yeatsian style.

Larkin himself acknowledged, both in his introduction to the reissued *The North Ship* in 1966, and in his 'Vernon Watkins: An Encounter and a Re-encounter' (collected in *Required Writing*), how powerful was the effect on him of Watkins's reading of Yeats to the Oxford University English Club in spring 1943, so that he 'spent the next three years trying to write like Yeats'. Many of the poems in *The North Ship* show the blended influence of Yeats and Watkins from 1943 until Larkin dispatched the typescript of that collection to the Fortune Press in November 1944.

The influence continues in many of the 1945–6 poems which Larkin added to some from *The North Ship* when making up the typescript collection of twenty-five poems with the title *In the Grip of Light* which he sent to the literary agent A. P. Watt late in 1947. This typescript survives, and its title page shows that it was rejected in 1948 by Faber and Faber, John Lane, J. M. Dent, Macmillan, Methuen, and John Lehmann. It contained, along with the Yeats- or Watkins-influenced poems, both 'Going' and 'Wedding-Wind'; and it seemed sensible to take this opportunity of filling in the missing pieces of what Larkin, in an interview in 1964, called 'a book with the portentous title of *In the Grip of Light*', if only to show how they relate, or do not relate, to their already known companions from *The North Ship*, *XX Poems*, and *The Less Deceived*.

Larkin's next attempt at publication was *XX Poems*, privately printed in Belfast in an edition of 100 copies in April 1951. Writing to Charles Madge in May 1950, Larkin enclosed thirteen poems ('a poor harvest from 6 years or so') together with a copy of *The North Ship*, and commented on the new poems: 'On the whole they seem much less poetic than the printed set, and much freer of the late Mr. W. B. Yeats also.' The thirteen poems included several which were to surface in *XX Poems*, and later in *The Less Deceived*, along with some that had had only periodical publication and three that have not until now been published. *XX Poems* itself was almost entirely ignored by the leading literary figures to whom Larkin sent it. But he had already begun to write the poems which were to establish his reputation.

Each poem is accompanied, whenever possible, by its completion date and, if published, its inclusion in a periodical, an anthology or a collection. Thus, for example, 'Heaviest of flowers, the head' (p.282) carries the notional date 1943–4, and an indication that it was first published in *Poetry from Oxford in Wartime* (February 1945), republished in *The North Ship* (July 1945), and included by Larkin in the typescript collection *In the*

Grip of Light in 1947. In the folder 'Unpublished Poems 1948- ' a small number carry Larkin's comment 'unfinished' on the typescripts. An even smaller number carry no such comment but clearly are unfinished, most obviously the ambitious poem 'The Dance', at which he worked with great concentration for over ten months in 1963–4 (there are more than forty pages of drafts in Notebook 6), but the cleanly typed version comes to an abrupt end after twelve eleven-line stanzas (see pp.154–8). All clearly unfinished poems, whether or not indicated as such by Larkin, are identified on the page in the present edition.

I have not included any poems which are more fragmentary. Among those thus excluded are: 'When I see Literature', written early in 1950, and addressed to a personified figure called 'Literature', who is bland, condescending, 'successful'; extensive drafts of a poem on the dates of coins and their significance to him (1935, 1941, 1946), written in the summer of 1954, just before the completion of 'Church Going'; attempts at four poems on the seasons, written at about the same time; a poem in complex stanza form, beginning 'Increasingly I think of them as young', which occupied him in the winter of 1962–3, and again in the summer of 1965; another attempt at a long poem, called 'The Duration', beginning 'It was like a war', which takes up fifteen pages of drafts between April and June 1969; and what was apparently his final struggle with a substantial poem, 'Letters to my mind', drafted in October and November 1979.

I have, a little regretfully, not included in the present edition any of the squibs, limericks and the like, which Larkin wrote in letters to his friends. Many of them will, in any case, appear in a volume of his *Selected Letters* which I am preparing, where they will be seen properly in context. They include such epigrams as these, dating from January 1954, the first called 'Love', the second 'Marriage':

> Not love you? Dear, I'd pay ten quid for you:
> Five down, and five when I got rid of you.

'My wife and I – we're *pals*. Marriage is *fun*.'
Yes: two can live as stupidly as one.

Much later, in 1977, there is part of what Larkin called 'an
unwritten Jubilee poem to HM', which begins:

After Healey's trading figures,
After Wilson's squalid crew . . .

Such a barbed couplet as his Black Paper effort (p.172) or such a
jeu d'esprit as 'Administration' (p.161) at least give a taste of this
side of Larkin.

To have added so many unpublished poems, from the flood at
the beginning to the trickle towards the end, together with
many others which he published in his lifetime but chose not to
collect, is something I do not take lightly. Philip Larkin's own
precise wishes in his will, drawn up during his illness in July
1985, were not at first entirely clear; yet he certainly gave his
literary executors, of whom I am one, discretion over the
publication of his unpublished manuscripts. I kept in mind the
fact that Larkin allowed his first book, which he ruefully
disowned, to be reissued over twenty years later; indeed,
anyone who has not read his introduction to the 1966 Faber and
Faber edition of *The North Ship* should do so now. He often
referred, if jocularly, to work which would have to be left for
'the posthumous volume' of his poems: '(Faber, Gollancz, Sun
Publications and Penthouse Ltd., 84 dollars – Eurodollars, I
should have said)'. He was, as I have indicated, scrupulous in
dating and preserving his notebooks and typescripts, and kept
a vigilant eye on the 'neglected responsibility' of the proper care
and retention of modern literary material. I believe that such a
man would not wish to stand in the way of a collected volume
such as this.

There is a sense in which a poet, when he dies, does (as
Auden wrote of Yeats) become his admirers. Larkin sometimes
feared, I think, that the appearance of what he considered to be
his inferior poems would encourage critics to tear his reputation

to pieces. In some cases, one can see why he chose not to publish, either at the time of writing or later; some poems he must have thought derivative, or too nakedly personal, or too raw, others simply not good enough. He was in many ways his own best, certainly most severe, critic. Few would claim – certainly I would not – that some of the poems first collected or first published here stand among Larkin's finest. Where the 1938–45 poems are concerned, I remind myself of Larkin's remarks in his preface to the Faber reissue of his first novel, *Jill*, about 'qualifying for the indulgence traditionally extended to juvenilia'. Yet the adolescent Audenesque of his schoolboy poems is astonishing and precocious, and deserves to be noticed.

Larkin as a young man had tried to publish several of the poems in the first section, had had them rejected, and had felt a failure. Today we can look at them, and him, differently. At the time of submitting *In the Grip of Light* at the end of 1947, he was in a state of extreme doubt and self-questioning, which was then made worse by the hammer-blows of successive rejections. Much later, when he had established a high reputation, he could not bring himself to publish anything about which he felt any doubt: he had been warned by his earlier failures. Many of his close friends were sent poems which he allowed them to read but which he wanted to have no wider circulation in his lifetime – even when those friends urged him to publish.

Some of the previously unpublished poems ('An April Sunday', 'The March Past', 'Mother, Summer, I', 'Far Out', 'Letter to a Friend about Girls', 'When first we faced', 'The Winter Palace', and several others, including the unfinished 'The Dance') deserve to stand with his best already known work. Taken together, as they should be, these collected poems show the growth of a major poet, testing, filtering, rejecting, modulating, achieving, before the dryness of his last years which he so regretted.

Anthony Thwaite

Abbreviations

An appendix lists, in the order Larkin assigned to them, the contents of each of the books and pamphlets published in his lifetime. The following abbreviations are used in the body of the book.

Poetry from Oxford in Wartime (1945) – POW
The North Ship (1945) – TNS
XX Poems (1951) – XX
The Fantasy Poets No. 21 (1954) – FP
The Less Deceived (1955) – TLD
The Whitsun Weddings (1964) – TWW
High Windows (1974) – HW

It also lists, in Larkin's order, the contents of the typescript of *In the Grip of Light* (1947) – ITGOL

Note on the Manuscripts and Typescripts

Of Philip Larkin's manuscript notebooks, the first (5 October 1944–10 March 1950) was presented by him in 1965 to the British Library, and is held there in the Department of Manuscripts as Add. MS 52619. The other seven notebooks are held by the Bodleian Library, Oxford, and are dated as follows:

2. 12 March 1950–September (?) 1951
3. 24 January 1953–24 May 1954
4. 10 June 1954–6 September 1958
5. Some early pages dated 11 November 1953 and 15 January 1955; then 19 September 1958–7 November 1960
6. 14 November 1960–12 May 1964
7. 6 October 1964–10 January 1972
8. 11 January 1972–26 November 1980

Along with these notebooks, the Bodleian Library also holds the seven 'little books' compiled by Larkin between 1939–42, the folder labelled 'Unpublished Poems 1948– ', and all the other manuscript and typescript material in Larkin's possession at the time of his death. This material is not available for unauthorized study or inspection at present.

There are very few variant readings or similar textual problems in Larkin's poems. The texts of these collected poems, both published and hitherto unpublished, have in each case been taken from the latest known version by the poet.

POEMS

1946–83

Going

There is an evening coming in
Across the fields, one never seen before,
That lights no lamps.

Silken it seems at a distance, yet
When it is drawn up over the knees and breast
It brings no comfort.

Where has the tree gone, that locked
Earth to the sky? What is under my hands,
That I cannot feel?

What loads my hands down?

February ? 1946 ITGOL (as 'Dying Day'), XX, TLD

Deep Analysis

I am a woman lying on a leaf;
  Leaf is silver, my flesh is golden,
Comely at all points, but I became your grief
  When you would not listen.

Through your one youth, whatever you pursued
  So singly, that I would be,
Desiring to kiss your arms and your straight side
  – Why would you not let me?

Why would you never relax, except for sleep,
  Face turned at the wall,
Denying the downlands, wheat, and the white sheep?
  And why was all

Your body sharpened against me, vigilant,
  Watchful, when all I meant
Was to make it bright, that it might stand
  Burnished before my tent?

I could not follow your wishes, but I know
  If they assuaged you
It would not be crying in this dark, your sorrow,
  It would not be crying, so

That my own heart drifts and cries, having no death
  Because of the darkness,
Having only your grief under my mouth
  Because of the darkness.

April 1946 ITGOL

[4]

'Come then to prayers'

Come then to prayers
And kneel upon the stone,
For we have tried
All courages on these despairs,
And are required lastly to give up pride,
And the last difficult pride in being humble.

Draw down the window-frame
That we may be unparted from the darkness,
Inviting to this house
Air from a field, air from a salt grave,
That questions if we have
Concealed no flaw in this confessional,
And, being satisfied,
Lingers, and troubles, and is lightless,
And so grows darker, as if clapped on a flame,
Whose great extinguishing still makes it tremble.

Only our hearts go beating towards the east.
Out of this darkness, let the unmeasured sword
Rising from sleep to execute or crown
Rest on our shoulders, as we then can rest
On the outdistancing, all-capable flood
Whose brim touches the morning. Down
The long shadows where undriven the dawn
Hunts light into nobility, arouse us noble.

13 May 1946 ITGOL

[5]

'And the wave sings because it is moving'

And the wave sings because it is moving;
Caught in its clear side, we also sing.

We are borne across graves, together, apart, together,
In the lifting wall imprisoned and protected,
And so devised to make ourselves unhappy.
Apart, we think we wish ourselves together,
Yet sue for solitude upon our meetings,
Till the unhindered turning of the sea
Changes our comforts into griefs greater
Than they were raised to cancel, breaking them.

Such are the sorrows that we search for meaning,
Such are the cries of birds across the waters,
Such are the mists the sun attacks at morning,
Laments, tears, wreaths, rocks, all ridden down
By the shout of the heart continually at work
To break with beating all our false devices;
Silver-tongued like a share it ploughs up failure,
Carries the night and day, fetches
Profit from sleep, from skies, driven or star-slung,
From all but death takes tithes,
Finds marrow in all but death to feed
And frame to us, but death it cannot invoke.

Death is a cloud alone in the sky with the sun.
Our hearts, turning like fish in the green wave,
Grow quiet in its shadow. For in the word death
There is nothing to grasp; nothing to catch or claim;
Nothing to adapt the skill of the heart to, skill
In surviving, for death it cannot survive,
Only resign the irrecoverable keys.
The wave falters and drowns. The coulter of joy

Breaks. The harrow of death
Deepens. And there are thrown up waves.

And the waves sing because they are moving.
And the waves sing above a cemetery of waters.

14 September 1946 ITGOL

Two Guitar Pieces

I

The tin-roofed shack by the railroad
Casts a shadow. Wheatstraws in the white dust
And a wagon standing. Stretched out into the sun
A dozen legs are idle in dungarees,
Dark hands and heads shaded from sun and working.
One frowns above a guitar: the notes, random
From tuning, wander into the heat
Like a new insect chirping in the scrub,
Untired at noon. A chord gathers and spills,
And a southern voice tails out around one note
Contentedly discontent.

                    Though the tracks
Burn to steel cities, they are taking
No one from these parts. Anyone could tell
Not even the wagon aims to go anywhere.

II

I roll a cigarette, and light
A spill at the stove. With a lungful of smoke
I join you at the window that has no curtain;
There we lean on the frame, and look
Below at the platz. A man is walking along
A path between the wreckage. And we stare at the dusk,
Sharing the cigarette.

              Behind us, our friend
Yawns, and collects the cards. The pack is short,
And dealing from now till morning would not bring
The highest hands. Besides, it's too dark to see.

[8]

So he kicks the stove, and lifts the guitar to his lap,
Strikes this note, that note.

                    I am trembling:
I am suddenly charged with their language, these six strings,
Suddenly made to see they can declare
Nothing but harmony, and may not move
Without a happy stirring of the air
That builds within this room a second room;
And the accustomed harnessing of grief
Tightens, because together or alone
We cannot trace that room; and then again
Because it is not a room, nor a world, but only
A figure spun on stirring of the air,
And so, untrue.

                    And so, I watch the square,
Empty again, like hunger after a meal.
You offer the cigarette and I say, Keep it,
Liking to see the glimmer come and go
Upon your face. What poor hands we hold,
When we face each other honestly! And now the guitar again,
Spreading me over the evening like a cloud,
Drifting, darkening: unable to bring rain.

        15 and 18 September 1946 ITGOL

The Dedicated

Some must employ the scythe
Upon the grasses,
That the walks be smooth
For the feet of the angel.
Some keep in repair
The locks, that the visitor
Unhindered passes
To the innermost chamber.

Some have for endeavour
To sign away life
As lover to lover,
Or a bird using its wings
To fly to the fowler's compass,
Not out of willingness,
But being aware of
Eternal requirings.

And if they have leave
To pray, it is for contentment
If the feet of the dove
Perch on the scythe's handle,
Perch once, and then depart
Their knowledge. After, they wait
Only the colder advent,
The quenching of candles.

18 September 1946 ITGOL (untitled), xx

Wedding-Wind

The wind blew all my wedding-day,
And my wedding-night was the night of the high wind;
And a stable door was banging, again and again,
That he must go and shut it, leaving me
Stupid in candlelight, hearing rain,
Seeing my face in the twisted candlestick,
Yet seeing nothing. When he came back
He said the horses were restless, and I was sad
That any man or beast that night should lack
The happiness I had.

                Now in the day
All's ravelled under the sun by the wind's blowing.
He has gone to look at the floods, and I
Carry a chipped pail to the chicken-run,
Set it down, and stare. All is the wind
Hunting through clouds and forests, thrashing
My apron and the hanging cloths on the line.
Can it be borne, this bodying-forth by wind
Of joy my actions turn on, like a thread
Carrying beads? Shall I be let to sleep
Now this perpetual morning shares my bed?
Can even death dry up
These new delighted lakes, conclude
Our kneeling as cattle by all-generous waters?

26 September 1946 ITGOL, XX, TLD

Träumerei

In this dream that dogs me I am part
Of a silent crowd walking under a wall,
Leaving a football match, perhaps, or a pit,
All moving the same way. After a while
A second wall closes on our right,
Pressing us tighter. We are now shut in
Like pigs down a concrete passage. When I lift
My head, I see the walls have killed the sun,
And light is cold. Now a giant whitewashed D
Comes on the second wall, but much too high
For them to recognise: I await the E,
Watch it approach and pass. By now
We have ceased walking and travel
Like water through sewers, steeply, despite
The tread that goes on ringing like an anvil
Under the striding A. I crook
My arm to shield my face, for we must pass
Beneath the huge, decapitated cross,
White on the wall, the T, and I cannot halt
The tread, the beat of it, it is my own heart,
The walls of my room rise, it is still night,
I have woken again before the word was spelt.

27 September 1946 ITGOL

[12]

To a Very Slow Air

The golden sheep are feeding, and
Their mouths harbour contentment;
Gladly my tongue praises
This hour scourged of dissension
By weight of their joyous fleeces.

The cloven hills are kneeling,
The sun such an anointment
Upon the forehead, on the hands and feet,
That all air is appointed
Our candid clothing, our elapsing state.

29 September 1946 ITGOL

'At the chiming of light upon sleep'

At the chiming of light upon sleep
A picture relapsed into the deep
Tarn, the hardly-stirring spring
Where memory changes to prefiguring.
Was it myself walking across that grass?
Was it myself, in a rank Michaelmas,
Closed among laurels? It was a green world,
Unchanging holly with the curled
Points, cypress and conifers,
All that through the winter bears
Coarsened fertility against the frost.
Nothing in such a sanctuary could be lost.
And yet, there were no flowers.

                  Morning, and more
Than morning, crosses the floor.
Have I been wrong, to think the breath
That sharpens life is life itself, not death?
Never to see, if death were killed,
No desperation, perpetually unfulfilled,
Would ever go fracturing down in ecstasy?
Death quarrels, and shakes the tree,
And fears are flowers, and flowers are generation,
And the founding, foundering, beast-instructed mansion
Of love called into being by this same death
Hangs everywhere its light. Unsheath
The life you carry and die, cries the cock
On the crest of the sun: unlock
The words and seeds that drove
Adam out of his undeciduous grove.

4 October 1946 ITGOL

[14]

'Many famous feet have trod'

Many famous feet have trod
Sublunary paths, and famous hands have weighed
The strength they have against the strength they need;
And famous lips interrogated God
Concerning franchise in eternity;
And in many differing times and places
Truth was attained (a moment's harmony);
Yet endless mornings break on endless faces:

Gold surf of the sun, each day
Exhausted through the world, gathers and whips
Irrevocably from eclipse;
The trodden way becomes the untrodden way,
We are born each morning, shelled upon
A sheet of light that paves
The palaces of sight, and brings again
The river shining through the field of graves.

Such renewal argues down
Our unsuccessful legacies of thought,
Annals of men who fought
Untiringly to change their hearts to stone,
Or to a wafer's poverty,
Or to a flower, but never tried to learn
The difficult triple sanity
Of being wafer, stone, and flower in turn.

Turn out your pockets on the tablecloth:
Consider what we know. A silver piece:
That's life; and, dealing in dichotomies,
This old discoloured copper coin is death.
Turn it about: it is impenetrable.
Reverse and obverse, neither bear

A sign or word remotely legible:
But spin the silver to a sphere,

Look in, and testify. Our mortal state
In turn is twisted in a double warp:
The light is waking and the dark is sleep
And twice a day before their gate
We kneel between them. There is more
Knowledge of sleep than death, and yet
Who knows the nature of our casting there,
Trawled inaccessible pool, or set

A line to haul its logic into speech?
Easier to balance on the hand
The waking that our senses can command,
For jewels are pebbles on a beach
Before this weaving, scattering, winged-and-footed
Privilege, this first, untold
And unrecurring luck that is never completed
Even in distance out of our hands' hold,

That makes, this waking traffic, this one last,
One paramount division. I declare
Two lineages electrify the air,
That will like pennons from a mast
Fly over sleep and life and death
Till sun is powerless to decoy
A single seed above the earth:
Lineage of sorrow: lineage of joy;

No longer think them aspects of the same;
Beyond each figured shield I trace
A different ancestry, a different face,
And sorrow must be held to blame
Because I follow it to my own heart
To find it feeding there on all that's bad:

It is sanctionable and right
Always to be ashamed of being sad.

Ashamed that sorrow's beckoned in
By each foiled weakness in the almanac
Engendered by the instinct-to-turn-back
– Which, if there are sins, should be called a sin –
Instinct that so worships my own face
It would halt time herewith
And put my wishes in its place:
And for this reason has great fear of death.

Because tides wound it;
The scuttling sand; the noose
Of what I have and shall lose,
Or have not and cannot get;
Partings in time or space
Wound it; it weeps sorely;
Holds sorrow before its face,
And all to pretend it is not part of me,

The blind part. I know what it will not know:
All stopping-up of cracks
Against dissolution builds a house of wax,
While years in wingspans go
Across and over our heads. Watch them:
They are flying east. They are flying to the ebb
Of dark. They are making sorrow seem
A spider busy on a forgotten web.

They are calling every fibre of the world
Into rejoicing, a mile-long silken cloth
Of wings moving lightwards out of death:
Lineage of joy into mortality hurled,
Endowing every actual bone
With motionless excitement. If quick feet

Must tread sublunary paths, attest this one:
Perpetual study to defeat

Each slovenly grief; the patience to expose
Untrue desire; assurance that, in sum,
Nothing's to reach, but something's to become,
That must be pitched upon the luminous,
Denying rest. Joy has no cause:
Though cut to pieces with a knife,
Cannot keep silence. What else should magnetize
Our drudging, hypocritical, ecstatic life?

15 *October 1946* ITGOL

Thaw

Tiny immortal streams are on the move:
The sun his hand uncloses like a statue,
Irrevocably: thereby such light is freed
That all the dingy hospital of snow
Dies back to ditches. Chalkbeds of heaven bear
These nameless tributaries, but they run
To earth. For here their pouring river reigns;
Here, busy with resurrection, sovereign waters
Confer among the roots, causing to fall
From patient memory forestfuls of grief.

How easily it falls, how easily I let drift
On the surface of morning feathers of self-reproach:
How easily I disperse the scolding of snow.

December ? 1946/early 1947 ITGOL

[19]

'Waiting for breakfast, while she brushed her hair'

Waiting for breakfast, while she brushed her hair,
I looked down at the empty hotel yard
Once meant for coaches. Cobblestones were wet,
But sent no light back to the loaded sky,
Sunk as it was with mist down to the roofs.
Drainpipes and fire-escape climbed up
Past rooms still burning their electric light:
I thought: Featureless morning, featureless night.

Misjudgment: for the stones slept, and the mist
Wandered absolvingly past all it touched,
Yet hung like a stayed breath; the lights burnt on,
Pin-points of undisturbed excitement; beyond the glass
The colourless vial of day painlessly spilled
My world back after a year, my lost lost world
Like a cropping deer strayed near my path again,
Bewaring the mind's least clutch. Turning, I kissed her,
Easily for sheer joy tipping the balance to love.

But, tender visiting,
Fallow as a deer or an unforced field,
How would you have me? Towards your grace
My promises meet and lock and race like rivers,
But only when you choose. Are you jealous of her?
Will you refuse to come till I have sent
Her terribly away, importantly live
Part invalid, part baby, and part saint?

15 December 1947 XX, TNS (1966)

'An April Sunday brings the snow'

An April Sunday brings the snow
Making the blossom on the plum trees green,
Not white. An hour or two, and it will go.
Strange that I spend that hour moving between

Cupboard and cupboard, shifting the store
Of jam you made of fruit from these same trees:
Five loads – a hundred pounds or more –
More than enough for all next summer's teas,

Which now you will not sit and eat.
Behind the glass, under the cellophane,
Remains your final summer – sweet
And meaningless, and not to come again.

4 April 1948

Neurotics

No one gives you a thought, as day by day
You drag your feet, clay-thick with misery.
None think how stalemate in you grinds away,
Holding your spinning wheels an inch too high
To bite on earth. The mind, it's said, is free:
But not your minds. They, rusted stiff, admit
Only what will accuse or horrify,
Like slot-machines only bent pennies fit.

So year by year your tense unfinished faces
Sink further from the light. No one pretends
To want to help you now. For interest passes
Always towards the young and more insistent,
And skirts locked rooms where a hired darkness ends
Your long defence against the non-existent.

March–April ? 1949

'I am washed upon a rock'

I am washed upon a rock
In an endless girding sea.
The sun is figured like a clock;
It turns and hangs at me.

My heart is ticking like the sun:
A lonely cloud drifts in the sky.
I dread its indecision.
If once it blocks the light, I die.

If I could make a single wish,
A bird might hover on the wing,
Within its beak a living fish,
And in the fish a wedding ring;

And when the ring was on my hand
The water would go down, and shrink
To harmless mirrors on the sand.
But to wish is first to think,

And to think is to be dumb,
And barren of a word to drop
That to a milder shore might come
And, years ahead, erect a crop.

18 March 1949

On Being Twenty-six

I feared these present years,
    The middle twenties,
When deftness disappears,
And each event is
Freighted with a source-encrusting doubt,
    And turned to drought.

I thought: this pristine drive
    Is sure to flag
At twenty-four or -five;
And now the slag
Of burnt-out childhood proves that I was right.
    What caught alight

Quickly consumed in me,
    As I foresaw.
Talent, felicity –
These things withdraw,
And are succeeded by a dingier crop
    That come to stop;

Or else, certainty gone,
    Perhaps the rest,
Tarnishing, linger on
As second-best.
Fabric of fallen minarets is trash.
    And in the ash

Of what has pleased and passed
    Is now no more
Than struts of greed, a last
Charred smile, a clawed
Crustacean hatred, blackened pride – of such
    I once made much.

And so, if I were sure
    I have no chance
To catch again that pure
Unnoticed stance,
I would calcine the outworn properties,
    Live on what is.

But it dies hard, that world;
    Or, being dead,
Putrescently is pearled,
For I, misled,
Make on my mind the deepest wound of all:
    Think to recall

At any moment, states
    Long since dispersed;
That if chance dissipates
The best, the worst
May scatter equally upon a touch.
    I kiss, I clutch,

Like a daft mother, putrid
    Infancy,
That can and will forbid
All grist to me
Except devaluing dichotomies:
    Nothing, and paradise.

May 1949

Modesties

Words as plain as hen-birds' wings
Do not lie,
Do not over-broider things –
Are too shy.

Thoughts that shuffle round like pence
Through each reign,
Wear down to their simplest sense,
Yet remain.

Weeds are not supposed to grow,
But by degrees
Some achieve a flower, although
No one sees.

13 May 1949 xx

'Sinking like sediment through the day'

Sinking like sediment through the day
To leave it clearer, onto the floor of the flask
(Vast summer vessel) settles a bitter carpet –
    Horror of life.

Huge awareness, elbowing vacancy,
Empty inside and out, replaces day.
(Like a fuse an impulse busily disintegrates
    Right back to its root.)

Out of the afternoon leans the indescribable woman:
'Embrace me, and I shall be beautiful' –
'Be beautiful, and I will embrace you' –
    We argue for hours.

13 May 1949

To Failure

You do not come dramatically, with dragons
That rear up with my life between their paws
And dash me butchered down beside the wagons,
The horses panicking; nor as a clause
Clearly set out to warn what can be lost,
What out-of-pocket charges must be borne,
Expenses met; nor as a draughty ghost
That's seen, some mornings, running down a lawn.

It is these sunless afternoons, I find,
Instal you at my elbow like a bore.
The chestnut trees are caked with silence. I'm
Aware the days pass quicker than before,
Smell staler too. And once they fall behind
They look like ruin. You have been here some time.

18 May 1949

At Grass

The eye can hardly pick them out
From the cold shade they shelter in,
Till wind distresses tail and mane;
Then one crops grass, and moves about
– The other seeming to look on –
And stands anonymous again.

Yet fifteen years ago, perhaps
Two dozen distances sufficed
To fable them: faint afternoons
Of Cups and Stakes and Handicaps,
Whereby their names were artificed
To inlay faded, classic Junes –

Silks at the start: against the sky
Numbers and parasols: outside,
Squadrons of empty cars, and heat,
And littered grass: then the long cry
Hanging unhushed till it subside
To stop-press columns on the street.

Do memories plague their ears like flies?
They shake their heads. Dusk brims the shadows.
Summer by summer all stole away,
The starting-gates, the crowds and cries –
All but the unmolesting meadows.
Almanacked, their names live; they

Have slipped their names, and stand at ease,
Or gallop for what must be joy,
And not a fieldglass sees them home,
Or curious stop-watch prophesies:
Only the groom, and the groom's boy,
With bridles in the evening come.

3 January 1950 XX, TLD

Compline

Behind the radio's altarlight
The hurried talk to God goes on:
Thy Kingdom come, Thy will be done,
Produce our lives beyond this night,
Open our eyes again to sun.

Unhindered in the dingy wards
Lives flicker out, one here, one there,
To send some weeping down the stair
With love unused, in unsaid words:
For this I would have quenched the prayer,

But for the thought that nature spawns
A million eggs to make one fish.
Better that endless notes beseech
As many nights, as many dawns,
If finally God grants the wish.

12 February 1950

Deceptions

'Of course I was drugged, and so heavily I did not regain my
consciousness till the next morning. I was horrified to discover that I
had been ruined, and for some days I was inconsolable, and cried
like a child to be killed or sent back to my aunt.' Mayhew, *London
Labour and the London Poor*

Even so distant, I can taste the grief,
Bitter and sharp with stalks, he made you gulp.
The sun's occasional print, the brisk brief
Worry of wheels along the street outside
Where bridal London bows the other way,
And light, unanswerable and tall and wide,
Forbids the scar to heal, and drives
Shame out of hiding. All the unhurried day
Your mind lay open like a drawer of knives.

Slums, years, have buried you. I would not dare
Console you if I could. What can be said,
Except that suffering is exact, but where
Desire takes charge, readings will grow erratic?
For you would hardly care
That you were less deceived, out on that bed,
Than he was, stumbling up the breathless stair
To burst into fulfilment's desolate attic.

20 February 1950 XX, TLD

Coming

On longer evenings,
Light, chill and yellow,
Bathes the serene
Foreheads of houses.
A thrush sings,
Laurel-surrounded
In the deep bare garden,
Its fresh-peeled voice
Astonishing the brickwork.
It will be spring soon,
It will be spring soon –
And I, whose childhood
Is a forgotten boredom,
Feel like a child
Who comes on a scene
Of adult reconciling,
And can understand nothing
But the unusual laughter,
And starts to be happy.

25 February 1950 XX, TLD

Fiction and the Reading Public

Give me a thrill, says the reader,
Give me a kick;
I don't care how you succeed, or
What subject you pick.
Choose something you know all about
That'll sound like real life:
Your childhood, your Dad pegging out,
How you sleep with your wife.

But that's not sufficient, unless
You make me feel good –
Whatever you're 'trying to express'
Let it be understood
That 'somehow' God plaits up the threads,
Makes 'all for the best',
That we may lie quiet in our beds
And not be 'depressed'.

For I call the tune in this racket:
I pay your screw,
Write reviews and the bull on the jacket –
So stop looking blue
And start serving up your sensations
Before it's too late;
Just please me for two generations –
You'll be 'truly great'.

25 February 1950 Essays in Criticism,
January 1954

How to Sleep

Child in the womb,
Or saint on a tomb –
Which way shall I lie
To fall asleep?
The keen moon stares
From the back of the sky,
The clouds are all home
Like driven sheep.

Bright drops of time,
One and two chime,
I turn and lie straight
With folded hands;
Convent-child, Pope,
They choose this state,
And their minds are wiped calm
As sea-levelled sands.

So my thoughts are:
But sleep stays as far,
Till I crouch on one side
Like a foetus again –
For sleeping, like death,
Must be won without pride,
With a nod from nature,
With a lack of strain,
And a loss of stature.

10 March 1950

Two Portraits of Sex

I Oils

Sun. Tree. Beginning. God in a thicket. Crown.
Never-abdicated constellation. Blood.
Barn-clutch of life. Trigger of the future.
Magic weed the doctor shakes in the dance.
Many rains and many rivers, making one river.
Password. Installation. Root of tongues.

Working-place to which the small seed is guided,
Inlet unvisited by marine biologist,
Entire alternative in man and woman
Opening at a touch like a water-flower,
New voice saying new words at a new speed
From which the future erupts like struck oil,

No one can migrate across your boundaries.
No one can exist without a habit for you.
No one can tear your thread out of himself.
No one can tie you down or set you free.
Apart from your tribe, there is only the dead,
And even them you grip and begin to use.

14 March 1950 xx

II Dry-Point

Endlessly, time-honoured irritant,
A bubble is restively forming at your tip.
Burst it as fast as we can –
It will grow again, until we begin dying.

[36]

Silently it inflates, till we're enclosed
And forced to start the struggle to get out:
Bestial, intent, real.
The wet spark comes, the bright blown walls collapse,

But what sad scapes we cannot turn from then:
What ashen hills! what salted, shrunken lakes!
How leaden the ring looks,
Birmingham magic all discredited,

And how remote that bare and sunscrubbed room,
Intensely far, that padlocked cube of light
We neither define nor prove,
Where you, we dream, obtain no right of entry.

17 March 1950 xx (as 'Etching'), TLD

The Literary World

I

'Finally, after five months of my life during which I could write nothing
that would have satisfied me, and for which no power will compensate
me . . .'

> My dear Kafka,
> When you've had five years of it, not five months,
> Five years of an irresistible force meeting an
>   immoveable object right in your belly,
> Then you'll know about depression.

II

> Mrs Alfred Tennyson
> Answered
>   begging letters
>   admiring letters
>   insulting letters
>   enquiring letters
>   business letters
>   and publishers' letters.
> She also
>   looked after his clothes
>   saw to his food and drink
>   entertained visitors
>   protected him from gossip and criticism
> And finally
>   (apart from running the household)
>   Brought up and educated the children.
>
> While all this was going on
> Mister Alfred Tennyson sat like a baby
> Doing his poetic business.

20 March 1950

Spring

Green-shadowed people sit, or walk in rings,
Their children finger the awakened grass,
Calmly a cloud stands, calmly a bird sings,
And, flashing like a dangled looking-glass,
Sun lights the balls that bounce, the dogs that bark,
The branch-arrested mist of leaf, and me,
Threading my pursed-up way across the park,
An indigestible sterility.

Spring, of all seasons most gratuitous,
Is fold of untaught flower, is race of water,
Is earth's most multiple, excited daughter;

And those she has least use for see her best,
Their paths grown craven and circuitous,
Their visions mountain-clear, their needs immodest.

19 May 1950 XX, TLD

Strangers

The eyes of strangers
Are cold as snowdrops,
Downcast, folded,
And seldom visited.

And strangers' acts
Cry but vaguely, drift
Across our attention's
Smoke-sieged afternoons.

And to live there, among strangers,
Calls for teashop behaviours:
Setting down the cup,
Leaving the right tip,

Keeping the soul unjostled,
The pocket unpicked,
The fancies lurid,
And the treasure buried.

20 May 1950

If, My Darling

If my darling were once to decide
Not to stop at my eyes,
But to jump, like Alice, with floating skirt into my head,

She would find no tables and chairs,
No mahogany claw-footed sideboards,
No undisturbed embers;

The tantalus would not be filled, nor the fender-seat cosy,
Nor the shelves stuffed with small-printed books for the
                                                        Sabbath,
Nor the butler bibulous, the housemaids lazy:

She would find herself looped with the creep of varying light,
Monkey-brown, fish-grey, a string of infected circles
Loitering like bullies, about to coagulate;

Delusions that shrink to the size of a woman's glove,
Then sicken inclusively outwards. She would also remark
The unwholesome floor, as it might be the skin of a grave,

From which ascends an adhesive sense of betrayal,
A Grecian statue kicked in the privates, money,
A swill-tub of finer feelings. But most of all

She'd be stopping her ears against the incessant recital
Intoned by reality, larded with technical terms,
Each one double-yolked with meaning and meaning's rebuttal:

For the skirl of that bulletin unpicks the world like a knot,
And to hear how the past is past and the future neuter
Might knock my darling off her unpriceable pivot.

23 May 1950 XX, TLD

Wants

Beyond all this, the wish to be alone:
However the sky grows dark with invitation-cards
However we follow the printed directions of sex
However the family is photographed under the flagstaff –
Beyond all this, the wish to be alone.

Beneath it all, desire of oblivion runs:
Despite the artful tensions of the calendar,
The life insurance, the tabled fertility rites,
The costly aversion of the eyes from death –
Beneath it all, desire of oblivion runs.

1 June 1950 XX, TLD

'Under a splendid chestnut tree'

Under a splendid chestnut tree
The rector clenched his fists
And swore that God exists,
Clamping his features stiff with certainty.
Twenty-five steps to the pond and ten to the hedge,
And his resolution had wilted round the edge,
Leaving him tilting a blind face to the sky,
Asking to die:
'To die, dear God, before a scum of doubt
Smear the whole universe, and smudge it out.'
Meanwhile the bees fumbled among the flowers,
The gardener smoked, the children poked about,
The cat lay on the baker's roof for hours.

Just then (but miles away) there knelt
A corpse-faced undergrad
Convinced that he was bad:
His soul was just a sink of filth, he felt.
Hare's eyes, staring across his prayer-locked hands,
Saw, not a washstand-set, but mammary glands;
All boyhood's treasure-trove, a *hortus siccus*
Of tits and knickers,
Baited his unused sex like tsetse flies,
Till, maddened, it charged out without disguise
And made the headlines. But the Gothic view
Was pricked with lamps and boys' street-distant cries,
Where chestnut-burrs dropped, bounced, and split in two.

Thus at the end of Shady Lane
A spinster eyed a fir
That meant to fall on her.
Watching it crouch and straighten and crouch again,
Her bright and childless eyes screwed up with dread.
And in the north a workman hugged his bed,

Hating the clouds, the stained unsightly breath
Of carious death.
Down centuries of streets they sit and listen
Where children chalk out games and gas-lights glisten,
Taking both voices in old arguments,
One plate, one cup, laid in the same position
For the departed lodger, innocence.

June 1950

'Who called love conquering'

Who called love conquering,
When its sweet flower
So easily dries among the sour
Lanes of the living?

Flowerless demonstrative weeds
Selfishly spread,
The white bride drowns in her bed
And tiny curled greeds

Grapple the sun down
By three o'clock
When the dire cloak of dark
Stiffens the town.

17 July 1950 xx

The Spirit Wooed

Once I believed in you,
    And then you came,
    Unquestionably new, as fame
Had said you were. But that was long ago.

You launched no argument,
    Yet I obeyed,
    Straightway, the instrument you played
Distant down sidestreets, keeping different time,

And never questioned what
    You fascinate
    In me; if good or not, the state
You pressed towards. There was no need to know.

Grave pristine absolutes
    Walked in my mind:
    So that I was not mute, or blind,
As years before or since. My only crime

Was holding you too dear.
    Was that the cause
    You daily came less near – a pause
Longer than life, if you decide it so?

1950?

No Road

Since we agreed to let the road between us
Fall to disuse,
And bricked our gates up, planted trees to screen us,
And turned all time's eroding agents loose,
Silence, and space, and strangers – our neglect
Has not had much effect.

Leaves drift unswept, perhaps; grass creeps unmown;
No other change.
So clear it stands, so little overgrown,
Walking that way tonight would not seem strange,
And still would be allowed. A little longer,
And time will be the stronger,

Drafting a world where no such road will run
From you to me;
To watch that world come up like a cold sun,
Rewarding others, is my liberty.
Not to prevent it is my will's fulfilment.
Willing it, my ailment.

28 October 1950 xx, TLD

Wires

The widest prairies have electric fences,
For though old cattle know they must not stray
Young steers are always scenting purer water
Not here but anywhere. Beyond the wires

Leads them to blunder up against the wires
Whose muscle-shredding violence gives no quarter.
Young steers become old cattle from that day,
Electric limits to their widest senses.

4 November 1950 XX, TLD

Absences

Rain patters on a sea that tilts and sighs.
Fast-running floors, collapsing into hollows,
Tower suddenly, spray-haired. Contrariwise,
A wave drops like a wall: another follows,
Wilting and scrambling, tirelessly at play
Where there are no ships and no shallows.

Above the sea, the yet more shoreless day,
Riddled by wind, trails lit-up galleries:
They shift to giant ribbing, sift away.

Such attics cleared of me! Such absences!

28 November 1950 TLD

'Since the majority of me'

Since the majority of me
Rejects the majority of you,
Debating ends forthwith, and we
Divide. And sure of what to do

We disinfect new blocks of days
For our majorities to rent
With unshared friends and unwalked ways.
But silence too is eloquent:

A silence of minorities
That, unopposed at last, return
Each night with cancelled promises
They want renewed. They never learn.

6 December 1950 xx

Arrival

Morning, a glass door, flashes
Gold names off the new city,
Whose white shelves and domes travel
The slow sky all day.
I land to stay here;
And the windows flock open
And the curtains fly out like doves
And the past dries in a wind.

Now let me lie down, under
A wide-branched indifference,
Shovel faces like pennies
Down the back of mind,
Find voices coined to
An argot of motor-horns,
And let the cluttered-up houses
Keep their thick lives to themselves.

For this ignorance of me
Seems a kind of innocence.
Fast enough I shall wound it:
Let me breathe till then
Its milk-aired Eden,
Till my own life impound it –
Slow-falling; grey-veil-hung; a theft,
A style of dying only.

1950 XX

Next, Please

Always too eager for the future, we
Pick up bad habits of expectancy.
Something is always approaching; every day
Till *then* we say,

Watching from a bluff the tiny, clear,
Sparkling armada of promises draw near.
How slow they are! And how much time they waste,
Refusing to make haste!

Yet still they leave us holding wretched stalks
Of disappointment, for, though nothing balks
Each big approach, leaning with brasswork prinked,
Each rope distinct,

Flagged, and the figurehead with golden tits
Arching our way, it never anchors; it's
No sooner present than it turns to past.
Right to the last

We think each one will heave to and unload
All good into our lives, all we are owed
For waiting so devoutly and so long.
But we are wrong:

Only one ship is seeking us, a black-
Sailed unfamiliar, towing at her back
A huge and birdless silence. In her wake
No waters breed or break.

16 January 1951 XX, TLD

[52]

Latest Face

Latest face, so effortless
Your great arrival at my eyes,
No one standing near could guess
Your beauty had no home till then;
Precious vagrant, recognise
My look, and do not turn again.

Admirer and admired embrace
On a useless level, where
I contain your current grace,
You my judgment; yet to move
Into real untidy air
Brings no lasting attribute –
Bargains, suffering, and love,
Not this always-planned salute.

Lies grow dark around us: will
The statue of your beauty walk?
Must I wade behind it, till
Something's found – or is not found –
Far too late for turning back?
Or, if I will not shift my ground,
Is your power actual – can
Denial of you duck and run,
Stay out of sight and double round,
Leap from the sun with mask and brand
And murder and not understand?

February 1951 XX, TLD

To My Wife

Choice of you shuts up that peacock-fan
The future was, in which temptingly spread
All that elaborative nature can.
Matchless potential! but unlimited
Only so long as I elected nothing;
Simply to choose stopped all ways up but one,
And sent the tease-birds from the bushes flapping.
No future now. I and you now, alone.

So for your face I have exchanged all faces,
For your few properties bargained the brisk
Baggage, the mask-and-magic-man's regalia.
Now you become my boredom and my failure,
Another way of suffering, a risk,
A heavier-than-air hypostasis.

19 March 1951

The March Past

The march interrupted the light afternoon.
Cars stopped dead, children began to run,
As out of the street-shadow into the sun

Discipline strode, music bullying aside
The credulous, prettily-coloured crowd,
Evoking an over-confident, over-loud

Holiday where the flags lisped and beckoned,
And all was focused, larger than we reckoned,
Into a consequence of thirty seconds.

The stamp and dash of surface sound cut short
Memory, intention, thought;
The vague heart sharpened to a candid court

Where exercised a sudden flock of visions:
Honeycombs of heroic separations,
Pure marchings, pure apparitions,

Until the crowd closed in behind.
Then music drooped. And what came back to mind
Was not its previous habit, but a blind

Astonishing remorse for things now ended
That of themselves were also rich and splendid
(But unsupported broke, and were not mended) –

Astonishing, for such things should be deep,
Rarely exhumable: not in a sleep
So light they can awake and occupy
An absent mind when any march goes by.

25 May 1951

[55]

Best Society

When I was a child, I thought,
Casually, that solitude
Never needed to be sought.
Something everybody had,
Like nakedness, it lay at hand,
Not specially right or specially wrong,
A plentiful and obvious thing
Not at all hard to understand.

Then, after twenty, it became
At once more difficult to get
And more desired – though all the same
More undesirable; for what
You are alone has, to achieve
The rank of fact, to be expressed
In terms of others, or it's just
A compensating make-believe.

Much better stay in company!
To love you must have someone else,
Giving requires a legatee,
Good neighbours need whole parishfuls
Of folk to do it on – in short,
Our virtues are all social; if,
Deprived of solitude, you chafe,
It's clear you're not the virtuous sort.

Viciously, then, I lock my door.
The gas-fire breathes. The wind outside
Ushers in evening rain. Once more
Uncontradicting solitude
Supports me on its giant palm;

And like a sea-anemone
Or simple snail, there cautiously
Unfolds, emerges, what I am.

1951?

'To put one brick upon another'

To put one brick upon another,
Add a third, and then a fourth,
Leaves no time to wonder whether
What you do has any worth.

But to sit with bricks around you
While the winds of heaven bawl
Weighing what you should or can do
Leaves no doubt of it at all.

1951?

'The local snivels through the fields'

The local snivels through the fields:
I sit between felt-hatted mums
Whose weekly day-excursion yields
Baby-sized parcels, bags of plums,
And bones of gossip good to clack
Past all the seven stations back.

Strange that my own elaborate spree
Should after fourteen days run out
In torpid rural company
Ignoring what my labels shout.
Death will be such another thing,
All we have done not mattering.

1951?

Unfinished Poem

I squeezed up the last stair to the room in the roof
And lay on the bed there with my jacket off.
Seeds of light were sown on the failure of evening.
The dew came down. I lay in the quiet, smoking.

That was a way to live – newspaper for sheets,
A candle and spirit stove, and a trouble of shouts
From below somewhere, a town smudgy with traffic!
That was a place to go, that emaciate attic!

For (as you will guess) it was death I had in mind,
Who covets our breath, who seeks and will always find;
To keep out of his thought was my whole care,
Yet down among sunlit courts, yes, he was there,

Taking his rents; yes, I had only to look
To see the shape of his head and the shine of his book,
And the creep of the world under his sparrow-trap sky,
To know how little slips his immortal memory.

So it was stale time then, day in, day out,
Blue fug in the room, nothing to do but wait
The start of his feet on the stair, that sad sound
Climbing to cut me from his restless mind

With a sign that the air should stick in my nose like bread,
The light swell up and turn black – so I shammed dead,
Still as a stuck pig, hoping he'd keep concerned
With boys who were making the fig when his back was turned;

And the sun and the stove and the mice and the gnawed paper
Made up the days and nights when I missed supper,
Paring my nails, looking over the farbelow street
Of tramways and bells. But one night I heard the feet.

Step after step they mounted with confidence.
Time shrank. They paused at the top. There was no defence.
I sprawled to my knees. Now they came straight at my door.
This, then, the famous eclipse? The crack in the floor

Widening for one long plunge? In a sharp trice,
The world, lifted and wrung, dripped with remorse.
The fact of breathing tightened into a shroud.
Light cringed. The door swung inwards. Over the threshold

Nothing like death stepped, nothing like death paused,
Nothing like death has such hair, arms so raised.
Why are your feet bare? Was not death to come?
Why is he not here? What summer have you broken from?

1951

[61]

Maturity

A stationary sense . . . as, I suppose,
I shall have, till my single body grows
     Inaccurate, tired;
Then I shall start to feel the backward pull
Take over, sickening and masterful –
     Some say, desired.

And this must be *the prime of life* . . . I blink,
As if at pain; for it is pain, to think
     This pantomime
Of compensating act and counter-act,
Defeat and counterfeit, makes up, in fact,
     My ablest time.

1951?

Marriages

When those of us who seem
Immodestly-accurate
Transcriptions of a dream
Are tired of singleness,
Their confidence will mate
Only with confidence –
With an equal candescence,
With a pregnant selfishness.

Not so with the remainder:
Frogmarched by old need
They chaffer for a partner –
Some undesirable,
With whom it is agreed
That words such as liberty,
Impulse, or beauty
Shall be unmentionable.

Scarecrows of chivalry
They strike strange bargains –
Adder-faced singularity
Espouses a nailed-up childhood,
Skin-disease pardons
Soft horror of living,
A gabble is forgiven
By chronic solitude.

So they are gathered in;
So they are not wasted,
As they would have been
By intelligent rancour,
An integrity of self-hatred.
Whether they forget
What they wanted first or not
They tarnish at quiet anchor.

12 June 1951

Arrivals, Departures

This town has docks where channel boats come sidling;
Tame water lanes, tall sheds, the traveller sees
(His bag of samples knocking at his knees),
And hears, still under slackened engines gliding,
His advent blurted to the morning shore.

And we, barely recalled from sleep there, sense
Arrivals lowing in a doleful distance –
Horny dilemmas at the gate once more.
Come and choose wrong, they cry, *come and choose wrong*;
And so we rise. At night again they sound,

Calling the traveller now, the outward bound:
O not for long, they cry, *O not for long* –
And we are nudged from comfort, never knowing
How safely we may disregard their blowing,
Or if, this night, happiness too is going.

24 January 1953 FP, TLD

He Hears that his Beloved has become Engaged
for C.G.B.

When she came on, you couldn't keep your seat;
Fighting your way up through the orchestra,
Tup-heavy bumpkin, you confused your feet,
Fell in the drum – how we went ha ha ha!
But once you gained her side and started waltzing
We all began to cheer; the way she leant
Her cheek on yours and laughed was so exalting
We thought you stooging for the management.

But no. What you did, any of us might.
And saying so I see our difference:
Not your aplomb (I used mine to sit tight),
But *fancying you improve her*. Where's the sense
In saying love, but meaning interference?
You'll only *change* her. Still, I'm sure you're right.

29 January 1953

Days

What are days for?
Days are where we live.
They come, they wake us
Time and time over.
They are to be happy in:
Where can we live but days?

Ah, solving that question
Brings the priest and the doctor
In their long coats
Running over the fields.

3 August 1953 TWW

Mother, Summer, I

My mother, who hates thunderstorms,
Holds up each summer day and shakes
It out suspiciously, lest swarms
Of grape-dark clouds are lurking there;
But when the August weather breaks
And rains begin, and brittle frost
Sharpens the bird-abandoned air,
Her worried summer look is lost.

And I her son, though summer-born
And summer-loving, none the less
Am easier when the leaves are gone;
Too often summer days appear
Emblems of perfect happiness
I can't confront: I must await
A time less bold, less rich, less clear:
An autumn more appropriate.

August 1953

'At thirty-one, when some are rich'

At thirty-one, when some are rich
And others dead,
I, being neither, have a job instead,
But come each evening back to a high room
Above deep gardenfuls of air, on which
Already has been laid an autumn bloom.

And here, instead of planning how
I can best thrive,
How best win fame and money while alive,
I sit down, supper over, and begin
One of the letters of a kind I now
Feel most of my spare time is going in:

I mean, letters to women – no,
Not of the sort
The papers tell us get read out in court,
Leading directly to or from the bed.
Love-letters only in a sense: they owe
Too much elsewhere to come under that head.

Too much to kindness, for a start;
I know, none better,
The eyelessness of days without a letter;
Too much to habit ('Stop? But why on earth . . .?'):
Too much to an unwillingness to part
With people wise enough to see my worth.

I'm kind, but not kinetic – don't
Enlist a word
Simply because its deed has been deferred;
Ends in themselves, my letters plot no change;
They carry nothing dutiable; they won't
Aspire, astound, establish or estrange.

[69]

Why write them, then? Are they in fact
Just compromise,
Amiable residue when each denies
The other's want? Or are they not so nice,
Stand-ins in each case simply for an act?
Mushrooms of virtue? or, toadstools of vice?

They taste the same. So summer ends,
And nights draw in.
Another evening wasted! I begin
Writing the envelope, and a bitter smoke
Of self-contempt, of boredom too, ascends.
What use is an endearment and a joke?

August 1953 ('unfinished')

Lines on a Young Lady's Photograph Album

At last you yielded up the album, which,
Once open, sent me distracted. All your ages
Matt and glossy on the thick black pages!
Too much confectionery, too rich:
I choke on such nutritious images.

My swivel eye hungers from pose to pose –
In pigtails, clutching a reluctant cat;
Or furred yourself, a sweet girl-graduate;
Or lifting a heavy-headed rose
Beneath a trellis, or in a trilby hat

(Faintly disturbing, that, in several ways) –
From every side you strike at my control,
Not least through these disquieting chaps who loll
At ease about your earlier days:
Not quite your class, I'd say, dear, on the whole.

But o, photography! as no art is,
Faithful and disappointing! that records
Dull days as dull, and hold-it smiles as frauds,
And will not censor blemishes
Like washing-lines, and Hall's-Distemper boards,

But shows the cat as disinclined, and shades
A chin as doubled when it is, what grace
Your candour thus confers upon her face!
How overwhelmingly persuades
That this is a real girl in a real place,

In every sense empirically true!
Or is it just *the past*? Those flowers, that gate,
These misty parks and motors, lacerate
Simply by being over; you
Contract my heart by looking out of date.

Yes, true; but in the end, surely, we cry
Not only at exclusion, but because
It leaves us free to cry. We know *what was*
Won't call on us to justify
Our grief, however hard we yowl across

The gap from eye to page. So I am left
To mourn (without a chance of consequence)
You, balanced on a bike against a fence;
To wonder if you'd spot the theft
Of this one of you bathing; to condense,

In short, a past that no one now can share,
No matter whose your future; calm and dry,
It holds you like a heaven, and you lie
Unvariably lovely there,
Smaller and clearer as the years go by.

18 September 1953 FP, TLD

Triple Time

This empty street, this sky to blandness scoured,
This air, a little indistinct with autumn
Like a reflection, constitute the present –
A time traditionally soured,
A time unrecommended by event.

But equally they make up something else:
This is the future furthest childhood saw
Between long houses, under travelling skies,
Heard in contending bells –
An air lambent with adult enterprise,

And on another day will be the past,
A valley cropped by fat neglected chances
That we insensately forbore to fleece.
On this we blame our last
Threadbare perspectives, seasonal decrease.

3 October 1953 TLD

Whatever Happened?

At once whatever happened starts receding.
Panting, and back on board, we line the rail
With trousers ripped, light wallets, and lips bleeding.

Yes, gone, thank God! Remembering each detail
We toss for half the night, but find next day
All's kodak-distant. Easily, then (though pale),

'Perspective brings significance,' we say,
Unhooding our photometers, and, snap!
What can't be printed can be thrown away.

Later, it's just a latitude: the map
Points out how unavoidable it was:
'Such coastal bedding always means mishap.'

Curses? The dark? Struggling? Where's the source
Of these yarns now (except in nightmares, of course)?

26 October 1953 FP, TLD

Autumn

The air deals blows: surely too hard, too often?
No: it is bent on bringing summer down.
Dead leaves desert in thousands, outwards, upwards,
Numerous as birds; but the birds fly away,

And the blows sound on, like distant collapsing water,
Or empty hospitals falling room by room
Down in the west, perhaps, where the angry light is.
Then rain starts; the year goes suddenly slack.

O rain, o frost, so much has still to be cleared:
All this ripeness, all this reproachful flesh,
And summer, that keeps returning like a ghost
Of something death has merely made beautiful,

And night skies so brilliantly spread-eagled
With their sharp hint of a journey – all must disperse
Before the season is lost and anonymous,
Like a London court one is never sure of finding

But none the less exists, at the back of the fog,
Bare earth, a lamp, scrapers. Then it will be time
To seek there that ill-favoured, curious house,
Bar up the door, mantle the fat flame,

And sit once more alone with sprawling papers,
Bitten-up letters, boxes of photographs,
And the case of butterflies so rich it looks
As if all summer settled there and died.

October 1953

Tops

Tops heel and yaw,
Sent newly spinning:
Squirm round the floor
At the beginning,
Then draw gravely up
Like candle-flames, till
They are soundless, asleep,
Moving, yet still.
So they run on,
Until, with a falter,
A flicker – soon gone –
Their pace starts to alter:
Heeling again
As if hopelessly tired
They wobble, and then
The poise we admired
Reels, clatters and sprawls,
Pathetically over.
– And what most appals
Is that tiny first shiver,
That stumble, whereby
We know beyond doubt
They have almost run out
And are starting to die.

24 October 1953 Listen,
Spring 1957

Hospital Visits

At length to hospital
This man was limited,
Where screens leant on the wall
And idle headphones hung.
Since he would soon be dead
They let his wife come along
And pour out tea, each day.

I don't know what was said;
Just hospital-talk,
As the bed was a hospital bed.
Then one day she fell
Outside on the sad walk
And her wrist broke – curable
At Outpatients, naturally.

Thereafter night and day
She came both for the sight
Of his slowing-down body
And for her own attending,
And there by day and night
With her blithe bone mending
Watched him in decay.

Winter had nearly ended
When he died (the screen was for that).
To make sure her wrist mended
They had her in again
To finish a raffia mat –
This meant (since it was begun
Weeks back) he died again as she came away.

4 December 1953

[77]

Autobiography at an Air-Station

Delay, well, travellers must expect
Delay. For how long? No one seems to know.
With all the luggage weighed, the tickets checked,
It can't be *long* . . . We amble to and fro,
Sit in steel chairs, buy cigarettes and sweets
And tea, unfold the papers. Ought we to smile,
Perhaps make friends? No: in the race for seats
You're best alone. Friendship is not worth while.

Six hours pass: if I'd gone by boat last night
I'd be there now. Well, it's too late for that.
The kiosk girl is yawning. I feel staled,
Stupefied, by inaction – and, as light
Begins to ebb outside, by fear; I set
So much on this Assumption. Now it's failed.

6 December 1953

Negative Indicative

Never to walk from the station's lamps and laurels
Carrying my father's lean old leather case
Crumbling like the register at the hotel;
Never to be shown upstairs

To a plain room smelling of soap, a towel
Neatly hung on the back of a rush chair,
The floor uneven, the grate choked with a frill,
Muslin curtains hiding the market square;

Never to visit the lame girl who lives three doors
Down Meeting-House Lane – 'This pile is ready; these
I shall finish tonight, with luck' – to watch, as she pours
Tea from a gold-lined jubilee pot, her eyes,

Her intelligent face; never, walking away
As light fails, to notice the first star
Pulsing alone in a long shell-coloured sky,
And remember the year has turned, and feel the air

Alive with the emblematic sound of water –

28 December 1953 ('unfinished')

Reasons for Attendance

The trumpet's voice, loud and authoritative,
Draws me a moment to the lighted glass
To watch the dancers – all under twenty-five –
Shifting intently, face to flushed face,
Solemnly on the beat of happiness.

– Or so I fancy, sensing the smoke and sweat,
The wonderful feel of girls. Why be out here?
But then, why be in there? Sex, yes, but what
Is sex? Surely, to think the lion's share
Of happiness is found by couples – sheer

Inaccuracy, as far as I'm concerned.
What calls me is that lifted, rough-tongued bell
(Art, if you like) whose individual sound
Insists I too am individual.
It speaks; I hear; others may hear as well,

But not for me, nor I for them; and so
With happiness. Therefore I stay outside,
Believing this; and they maul to and fro,
Believing that; and both are satisfied,
If no one has misjudged himself. Or lied.

30 December 1953 TLD

[80]

I Remember, I Remember

Coming up England by a different line
For once, early in the cold new year,
We stopped, and, watching men with number-plates
Sprint down the platform to familiar gates,
'Why, Coventry!' I exclaimed. 'I was born here.'

I leant far out, and squinnied for a sign
That this was still the town that had been 'mine'
So long, but found I wasn't even clear
Which side was which. From where those cycle-crates
Were standing, had we annually departed

For all those family hols? . . . A whistle went:
Things moved. I sat back, staring at my boots.
'Was that,' my friend smiled, 'where you "have your roots"?'
No, only where my childhood was unspent,
I wanted to retort, just where I started:

By now I've got the whole place clearly charted.
Our garden, first: where I did not invent
Blinding theologies of flowers and fruits,
And wasn't spoken to by an old hat.
And here we have that splendid family

I never ran to when I got depressed,
The boys all biceps and the girls all chest,
Their comic Ford, their farm where I could be
'Really myself'. I'll show you, come to that,
The bracken where I never trembling sat,

Determined to go through with it; where she
Lay back, and 'all became a burning mist'.
And, in those offices, my doggerel
Was not set up in blunt ten-point, nor read
By a distinguished cousin of the mayor,

Who didn't call and tell my father *There*
Before us, had we the gift to see ahead –
'You look as if you wished the place in Hell,'
My friend said, 'judging from your face.' 'Oh well,
I suppose it's not the place's fault,' I said.

'Nothing, like something, happens anywhere.'

8 January 1954 TLD

For Sidney Bechet

That note you hold, narrowing and rising, shakes
Like New Orleans reflected on the water,
And in all ears appropriate falsehood wakes,

Building for some a legendary Quarter
Of balconies, flower-baskets and quadrilles,
Everyone making love and going shares –

Oh, play that thing! Mute glorious Storyvilles
Others may license, grouping round their chairs
Sporting-house girls like circus tigers (priced

Far above rubies) to pretend their fads,
While scholars *manqués* nod around unnoticed
Wrapped up in personnels like old plaids.

On me your voice falls as they say love should,
Like an enormous yes. My Crescent City
Is where your speech alone is understood,

And greeted as the natural noise of good,
Scattering long-haired grief and scored pity.

15 January 1954 TWW

[83]

Born Yesterday
for Sally Amis

Tightly-folded bud,
I have wished you something
None of the others would:
Not the usual stuff
About being beautiful,
Or running off a spring
Of innocence and love –
They will all wish you that,
And should it prove possible,
Well, you're a lucky girl.

But if it shouldn't, then
May you be ordinary;
Have, like other women,
An average of talents:
Not ugly, not good-looking,
Nothing uncustomary
To pull you off your balance,
That, unworkable itself,
Stops all the rest from working.
In fact, may you be dull –
If that is what a skilled,
Vigilant, flexible,
Unemphasised, enthralled
Catching of happiness is called.

20 January 1954 TLD

Poetry of Departures

Sometimes you hear, fifth-hand,
As epitaph:
He chucked up everything
And just cleared off,
And always the voice will sound
Certain you approve
This audacious, purifying,
Elemental move.

And they are right, I think.
We all hate home
And having to be there:
I detest my room,
Its specially-chosen junk,
The good books, the good bed,
And my life, in perfect order:
So to hear it said

He walked out on the whole crowd
Leaves me flushed and stirred,
Like *Then she undid her dress*
Or *Take that you bastard;*
Surely I can, if he did?
And that helps me stay
Sober and industrious.
But I'd go today,

Yes, swagger the nut-strewn roads,
Crouch in the fo'c'sle
Stubbly with goodness, if
It weren't so artificial,
Such a deliberate step backwards

To create an object:
Books; china; a life
Reprehensibly perfect.

23 January 1954 TLD

Midwinter Waking

Paws there. Snout there as well. Mustiness. Mould.
Darkness; a desire to stretch, to scratch.
Then has the – ? Then is it – ? Nudge the thatch,
Displace the stiffened leaves: look out. How cold,
How dried a stillness. Like a blade on stone,
A wind is scraping, first this way, then that.
Morning, perhaps; but not a proper one.
Turn. Sleep will unshell us, but not yet.

27 January 1954

Success Story

To fail (transitive and intransitive)
I find to mean *be missing, disappoint*,
Or *not succeed in the attainment of*
(As in this case, *f. to do what I want*);
They trace it from the Latin *to deceive* . . .

Yes. But it wasn't that I played unfair:
Under fourteen, I sent in six words
My Chief Ambition to the Editor
With the signed promise about afterwards –
I undertake rigidly to forswear

The diet of this world, all rich game
And fat forbidding fruit, go by the board
Until – But that *until* has never come,
And I am starving where I always did.
Time to fall to, I fancy: long past time.

The explanation goes like this, in daylight:
To be ambitious is to fall in love
With a particular life you haven't got
And (since love picks your opposite) won't achieve.
That's clear as day. But come back late at night,

You'll hear a curious counter-whispering:
Success, it says, you've scored a great success.
Your wish has flowered, you've dodged the dirty feeding,
Clean past it now at hardly any price –
Just some pretence about the other thing.

11 March 1954 The Grapevine, February 1957

Toads

Why should I let the toad *work*
    Squat on my life?
Can't I use my wit as a pitchfork
    And drive the brute off?

Six days of the week it soils
    With its sickening poison –
Just for paying a few bills!
    That's out of proportion.

Lots of folk live on their wits:
    Lecturers, lispers,
Losels, loblolly-men, louts –
    They don't end as paupers;

Lots of folk live up lanes
    With fires in a bucket,
Eat windfalls and tinned sardines –
    They seem to like it.

Their nippers have got bare feet,
    Their unspeakable wives
Are skinny as whippets – and yet
    No one actually *starves*.

Ah, were I courageous enough
    To shout *Stuff your pension!*
But I know, all too well, that's the stuff
    That dreams are made on:

For something sufficiently toad-like
    Squats in me, too;
Its hunkers are heavy as hard luck,
    And cold as snow,

And will never allow me to blarney
    My way to getting
The fame and the girl and the money
    All at one sitting.

I don't say, one bodies the other
    One's spiritual truth;
But I do say it's hard to lose either,
    When you have both.

16 March 1954 TLD

Gathering Wood

On short, still days
  At the shut of the year
We search the pathways
  Where the coverts were.

For kindling-wood we come,
  And make up bundles,
Carrying them home
  Down long low tunnels.

Soon air-frosts haze
  Snow-thickened shires;
O short, still days!
  O burrow fires!

25 March 1954

Skin

Obedient daily dress,
You cannot always keep
That unfakable young surface.
You must learn your lines –
Anger, amusement, sleep;
Those few forbidding signs

Of the continuous coarse
Sand-laden wind, time;
You must thicken, work loose
Into an old bag
Carrying a soiled name.
Parch then; be roughened; sag;

And pardon me, that I
Could find, when you were new,
No brash festivity
To wear you at, such as
Clothes are entitled to
Till the fashion changes.

5 April 1954 TLD

Water

If I were called in
To construct a religion
I should make use of water.

Going to church
Would entail a fording
To dry, different clothes;

My liturgy would employ
Images of sousing,
A furious devout drench,

And I should raise in the east
A glass of water
Where any-angled light
Would congregate endlessly.

6 April 1954 TWW

Continuing to Live

Continuing to live – that is, repeat
A habit formed to get necessaries –
Is nearly always losing, or going without.
    It varies.

This loss of interest, hair, and enterprise –
Ah, if the game were poker, yes,
You might discard them, draw a full house!
    But it's chess.

And once you have walked the length of your mind, what
You command is clear as a lading-list.
Anything else must not, for you, be thought
    To exist.

And what's the profit? Only that, in time,
We half-identify the blind impress
All our behavings bear, may trace it home.
    But to confess,

On that green evening when our death begins,
Just what it was, is hardly satisfying,
Since it applied only to one man once,
    And that one dying.

24 April 1954 A Keepsake for the New Library, 1973

Age

My age fallen away like white swaddling
Floats in the middle distance, becomes
An inhabited cloud. I bend closer, discern
A lighted tenement scuttling with voices.
O you tall game I tired myself with joining!
Now I wade through you like knee-level weeds,

And they attend me, dear translucent bergs:
Silence and space. By now so much has flown
From the nest here of my head that I needs must turn
To know what prints I leave, whether of feet,
Or spoor of pads, or a bird's adept splay.

26 May 1954 TLD

'Long roots moor summer to our side of earth'

Long roots moor summer to our side of earth.
I wake: already taller than the green
River-fresh castles of unresting leaf
Where loud birds dash,
It unfolds upward a long breadth, a shine

Wherein all seeds and clouds and winged things
Employ the many-levelled acreage.
Absence with absence makes a travelling angle,
And pressure of the sun
In silence sleeps like equiloaded scales.

Where can I turn except away, knowing
Myself outdistanced, out-invented? what
Reply can the vast flowering strike from us,
Unless it be the one
You make today in London: to be married?

12 June 1954

Church Going

Once I am sure there's nothing going on
I step inside, letting the door thud shut.
Another church: matting, seats, and stone,
And little books; sprawlings of flowers, cut
For Sunday, brownish now; some brass and stuff
Up at the holy end; the small neat organ;
And a tense, musty, unignorable silence,
Brewed God knows how long. Hatless, I take off
My cycle-clips in awkward reverence,

Move forward, run my hand around the font.
From where I stand, the roof looks almost new –
Cleaned, or restored? Someone would know: I don't.
Mounting the lectern, I peruse a few
Hectoring large-scale verses, and pronounce
'Here endeth' much more loudly than I'd meant.
The echoes snigger briefly. Back at the door
I sign the book, donate an Irish sixpence,
Reflect the place was not worth stopping for.

Yet stop I did: in fact I often do,
And always end much at a loss like this,
Wondering what to look for; wondering, too,
When churches fall completely out of use
What we shall turn them into, if we shall keep
A few cathedrals chronically on show,
Their parchment, plate and pyx in locked cases,
And let the rest rent-free to rain and sheep.
Shall we avoid them as unlucky places?

Or, after dark, will dubious women come
To make their children touch a particular stone;
Pick simples for a cancer; or on some
Advised night see walking a dead one?

Power of some sort or other will go on
In games, in riddles, seemingly at random;
But superstition, like belief, must die,
And what remains when disbelief has gone?
Grass, weedy pavement, brambles, buttress, sky,

A shape less recognisable each week,
A purpose more obscure. I wonder who
Will be the last, the very last, to seek
This place for what it was; one of the crew
That tap and jot and know what rood-lofts were?
Some ruin-bibber, randy for antique,
Or Christmas-addict, counting on a whiff
Of gown-and-bands and organ-pipes and myrrh?
Or will he be my representative,

Bored, uninformed, knowing the ghostly silt
Dispersed, yet tending to this cross of ground
Through suburb scrub because it held unspilt
So long and equably what since is found
Only in separation – marriage, and birth,
And death, and thoughts of these – for which was built
This special shell? For, though I've no idea
What this accoutred frowsty barn is worth,
It pleases me to stand in silence here;

A serious house on serious earth it is,
In whose blent air all our compulsions meet,
Are recognised, and robed as destinies.
And that much never can be obsolete,
Since someone will forever be surprising
A hunger in himself to be more serious,
And gravitating with it to this ground,
Which, he once heard, was proper to grow wise in,
If only that so many dead lie round.

28 July 1954 TLD

[98]

Places, Loved Ones

No, I have never found
The place where I could say
This is my proper ground,
Here I shall stay;
Nor met that special one
Who has an instant claim
On everything I own
Down to my name;

To find such seems to prove
You want no choice in where
To build, or whom to love;
You ask them to bear
You off irrevocably,
So that it's not your fault
Should the town turn dreary,
The girl a dolt.

Yet, having missed them, you're
Bound, none the less, to act
As if what you settled for
Mashed you, in fact;
And wiser to keep away
From thinking you still might trace
Uncalled-for to this day
Your person, your place.

10 October 1954 TLD

Myxomatosis

Caught in the centre of a soundless field
While hot inexplicable hours go by
What trap is this? Where were its teeth concealed?
You seem to ask.
                  I make a sharp reply,
Then clean my stick. I'm glad I can't explain
Just in what jaws you were to suppurate:
You may have thought things would come right again
If you could only keep quite still and wait.

1954 TLD

Washing at their identity.
Now, helpless in the hollow of
An unarmorial age, a trough
Of smoke in slow suspended skeins
Above their scrap of history,
Only an attitude remains:

Time has transfigured them into
Untruth. The stone fidelity
They hardly meant has come to be
Their final blazon, and to prove
Our almost-instinct almost true:
What will survive of us is love.

20 February 1956 TWW

First Sight

Lambs that learn to walk in snow
When their bleating clouds the air
Meet a vast unwelcome, know
Nothing but a sunless glare.
Newly stumbling to and fro
All they find, outside the fold,
Is a wretched width of cold.

As they wait beside the ewe,
Her fleeces wetly caked, there lies
Hidden round them, waiting too,
Earth's immeasurable surprise.
They could not grasp it if they knew,
What so soon will wake and grow
Utterly unlike the snow.

3 March 1956 TWW

Love Songs in Age

She kept her songs, they took so little space,
   The covers pleased her:
One bleached from lying in a sunny place,
One marked in circles by a vase of water,
One mended, when a tidy fit had seized her,
   And coloured, by her daughter –
So they had waited, till in widowhood
She found them, looking for something else, and stood

Relearning how each frank submissive chord
   Had ushered in
Word after sprawling hyphenated word,
And the unfailing sense of being young
Spread out like a spring-woken tree, wherein
   That hidden freshness sung,
That certainty of time laid up in store
As when she played them first. But, even more,

The glare of that much-mentioned brilliance, love,
   Broke out, to show
Its bright incipience sailing above,
Still promising to solve, and satisfy,
And set unchangeably in order. So
   To pile them back, to cry,
Was hard, without lamely admitting how
It had not done so then, and could not now.

1 January 1957 TWW

[113]

The Whitsun Weddings

That Whitsun, I was late getting away:
    Not till about
One-twenty on the sunlit Saturday
Did my three-quarters-empty train pull out,
All windows down, all cushions hot, all sense
Of being in a hurry gone. We ran
Behind the backs of houses, crossed a street
Of blinding windscreens, smelt the fish-dock; thence
The river's level drifting breadth began,
Where sky and Lincolnshire and water meet.

All afternoon, through the tall heat that slept
    For miles inland,
A slow and stopping curve southwards we kept.
Wide farms went by, short-shadowed cattle, and
Canals with floatings of industrial froth;
A hothouse flashed uniquely: hedges dipped
And rose: and now and then a smell of grass
Displaced the reek of buttoned carriage-cloth
Until the next town, new and nondescript,
Approached with acres of dismantled cars.

At first, I didn't notice what a noise
    The weddings made
Each station that we stopped at: sun destroys
The interest of what's happening in the shade,
And down the long cool platforms whoops and skirls
I took for porters larking with the mails,
And went on reading. Once we started, though,
We passed them, grinning and pomaded, girls
In parodies of fashion, heels and veils,
All posed irresolutely, watching us go,

As if out on the end of an event
  Waving goodbye
To something that survived it. Struck, I leant
More promptly out next time, more curiously,
And saw it all again in different terms:
The fathers with broad belts under their suits
And seamy foreheads; mothers loud and fat;
An uncle shouting smut; and then the perms,
The nylon gloves and jewellery-substitutes,
The lemons, mauves, and olive-ochres that

Marked off the girls unreally from the rest.
  Yes, from cafés
And banquet-halls up yards, and bunting-dressed
Coach-party annexes, the wedding-days
Were coming to an end. All down the line
Fresh couples climbed aboard: the rest stood round;
The last confetti and advice were thrown,
And, as we moved, each face seemed to define
Just what it saw departing: children frowned
At something dull; fathers had never known

Success so huge and wholly farcical;
  The women shared
The secret like a happy funeral;
While girls, gripping their handbags tighter, stared
At a religious wounding. Free at last,
And loaded with the sum of all they saw,
We hurried towards London, shuffling gouts of steam.
Now fields were building-plots, and poplars cast
Long shadows over major roads, and for
Some fifty minutes, that in time would seem

Just long enough to settle hats and say
  I nearly died,
A dozen marriages got under way.
They watched the landscape, sitting side by side
– An Odeon went past, a cooling tower,
And someone running up to bowl – and none
Thought of the others they would never meet
Or how their lives would all contain this hour.
I thought of London spread out in the sun,
Its postal districts packed like squares of wheat:

There we were aimed. And as we raced across
  Bright knots of rail
Past standing Pullmans, walls of blackened moss
Came close, and it was nearly done, this frail
Travelling coincidence; and what it held
Stood ready to be loosed with all the power
That being changed can give. We slowed again,
And as the tightened brakes took hold, there swelled
A sense of falling, like an arrow-shower
Sent out of sight, somewhere becoming rain.

18 October 1958 TWW

Self's the Man

Oh, no one can deny
That Arnold is less selfish than I.
He married a woman to stop her getting away
Now she's there all day,

And the money he gets for wasting his life on work
She takes as her perk
To pay for the kiddies' clobber and the drier
And the electric fire,

And when he finishes supper
Planning to have a read at the evening paper
It's *Put a screw in this wall* –
He has no time at all,

With the nippers to wheel round the houses
And the hall to paint in his old trousers
And that letter to her mother
Saying *Won't you come for the summer.*

To compare his life and mine
Makes me feel a swine:
Oh, no one can deny
That Arnold is less selfish than I.

But wait, not so fast:
Is there such a contrast?
He was out for his own ends
Not just pleasing his friends;

And if it was such a mistake
He still did it for his own sake,
Playing his own game.
So he and I are the same,

Only I'm a better hand
At knowing what I can stand
Without them sending a van –
Or I suppose I can.

5 November 1958 TWW

Home is so Sad

Home is so sad. It stays as it was left,
Shaped to the comfort of the last to go
As if to win them back. Instead, bereft
Of anyone to please, it withers so,
Having no heart to put aside the theft

And turn again to what it started as,
A joyous shot at how things ought to be,
Long fallen wide. You can see how it was:
Look at the pictures and the cutlery.
The music in the piano stool. That vase.

31 December 1958 TWW

Far Out

Beyond the bright cartoons
Are darker spaces where
Small cloudy nests of stars
Seem to float on the air.

These have no proper names:
Men out alone at night
Never look up at them
For guidance or delight,

For such evasive dust
Can make so little clear:
Much less is known than not,
More far than near.

1 February 1959

Afternoons

Summer is fading:
The leaves fall in ones and twos
From trees bordering
The new recreation ground.
In the hollows of afternoons
Young mothers assemble
At swing and sandpit
Setting free their children.

Behind them, at intervals,
Stand husbands in skilled trades,
An estateful of washing,
And the albums, lettered
Our Wedding, lying
Near the television:
Before them, the wind
Is ruining their courting-places

That are still courting-places
(But the lovers are all in school),
And their children, so intent on
Finding more unripe acorns,
Expect to be taken home.
Their beauty has thickened.
Something is pushing them
To the side of their own lives.

September ? 1959 TWW

[121]

Letter to a Friend about Girls

After comparing lives with you for years
I see how I've been losing: all the while
I've met a different gauge of girl from yours.
Grant that, and all the rest makes sense as well:
My mortification at your pushovers,
Your mystification at my fecklessness –
Everything proves we play in separate leagues.
Before, I couldn't credit your intrigues
Because I thought all girls the same, but yes,
You bag real birds, though they're from alien covers.

Now I believe your staggering skirmishes
In train, tutorial and telephone booth,
The wife whose husband watched away matches
While she behaved so badly in a bath,
And all the rest who beckon from that world
Described on Sundays only, where to want
Is straightway to be wanted, seek to find,
And no one gets upset or seems to mind
At what you say to them, or what you don't:
A world where all the nonsense is annulled,

And beauty is accepted slang for yes.
But equally, haven't you noticed mine?
They have their world, not much compared with yours,
But where they work, and age, and put off men
By being unattractive, or too shy,
Or having morals – anyhow, none give in:
Some of them go quite rigid with disgust
At anything but marriage: that's all lust
And so not worth considering; they begin
Fetching your hat, so that you have to lie

Till everything's confused: you mine away
For months, both of you, till the collapse comes
Into remorse, tears, and wondering why
You ever start such boring barren games
– But there, don't mind my *saeva indignatio*:
I'm happier now I've got things clear, although
It's strange we never meet each other's sort:
There should be equal chances, I'd've thought.
Must finish now. One day perhaps I'll know
What makes you be so lucky in your ratio

– One of those 'more things', could it be? *Horatio.*

December 1959

'None of the books have time'

None of the books have time
To say how being selfless feels,
They make it sound a superior way
Of getting what you want. It isn't at all.

Selflessness is like waiting in a hospital
In a badly-fitting suit on a cold wet morning.
Selfishness is like listening to good jazz
With drinks for further orders and a huge fire.

1 January 1960

As Bad as a Mile

Watching the shied core
Striking the basket, skidding across the floor,
Shows less and less of luck, and more and more

Of failure spreading back up the arm
Earlier and earlier, the unraised hand calm,
The apple unbitten in the palm.

9 February 1960 TWW

Faith Healing

Slowly the women file to where he stands
Upright in rimless glasses, silver hair,
Dark suit, white collar. Stewards tirelessly
Persuade them onwards to his voice and hands,
Within whose warm spring rain of loving care
Each dwells some twenty seconds. *Now, dear child,*
What's wrong, the deep American voice demands,
And, scarcely pausing, goes into a prayer
Directing God about this eye, that knee.
Their heads are clasped abruptly; then, exiled

Like losing thoughts, they go in silence; some
Sheepishly stray, not back into their lives
Just yet; but some stay stiff, twitching and loud
With deep hoarse tears, as if a kind of dumb
And idiot child within them still survives
To re-awake at kindness, thinking a voice
At last calls them alone, that hands have come
To lift and lighten; and such joy arrives
Their thick tongues blort, their eyes squeeze grief, a crowd
Of huge unheard answers jam and rejoice –

What's wrong! Moustached in flowered frocks they shake:
By now, all's wrong. In everyone there sleeps
A sense of life lived according to love.
To some it means the difference they could make
By loving others, but across most it sweeps
As all they might have done had they been loved.
That nothing cures. An immense slackening ache,
As when, thawing, the rigid landscape weeps,
Spreads slowly through them – that, and the voice above
Saying *Dear child*, and all time has disproved.

10 May 1960 TWW

[126]

MCMXIV

Those long uneven lines
Standing as patiently
As if they were stretched outside
The Oval or Villa Park,
The crowns of hats, the sun
On moustached archaic faces
Grinning as if it were all
An August Bank Holiday lark;

And the shut shops, the bleached
Established names on the sunblinds,
The farthings and sovereigns,
And dark-clothed children at play
Called after kings and queens,
The tin advertisements
For cocoa and twist, and the pubs
Wide open all day;

And the countryside not caring:
The place-names all hazed over
With flowering grasses, and fields
Shadowing Domesday lines
Under wheat's restless silence;
The differently-dressed servants
With tiny rooms in huge houses,
The dust behind limousines;

Never such innocence,
Never before or since,
As changed itself to past
Without a word – the men
Leaving the gardens tidy,

The thousands of marriages
Lasting a little while longer:
Never such innocence again.

17 May 1960 TWW

Talking in Bed

Talking in bed ought to be easiest,
Lying together there goes back so far,
An emblem of two people being honest.

Yet more and more time passes silently.
Outside, the wind's incomplete unrest
Builds and disperses clouds about the sky,

And dark towns heap up on the horizon.
None of this cares for us. Nothing shows why
At this unique distance from isolation

It becomes still more difficult to find
Words at once true and kind,
Or not untrue and not unkind.

10 August 1960 TWW

Take One Home for the Kiddies

On shallow straw, in shadeless glass,
Huddled by empty bowls, they sleep:
No dark, no dam, no earth, no grass –
Mam, get us one of them to keep.

Living toys are something novel,
But it soon wears off somehow.
Fetch the shoebox, fetch the shovel –
Mam, we're playing funerals now.

13 *August 1960* TWW

A Study of Reading Habits

When getting my nose in a book
Cured most things short of school,
It was worth ruining my eyes
To know I could still keep cool,
And deal out the old right hook
To dirty dogs twice my size.

Later, with inch-thick specs,
Evil was just my lark:
Me and my cloak and fangs
Had ripping times in the dark.
The women I clubbed with sex!
I broke them up like meringues.

Don't read much now: the dude
Who lets the girl down before
The hero arrives, the chap
Who's yellow and keeps the store,
Seem far too familiar. Get stewed:
Books are a load of crap.

20 August 1960   TWW

Ambulances

Closed like confessionals, they thread
Loud noons of cities, giving back
None of the glances they absorb.
Light glossy grey, arms on a plaque,
They come to rest at any kerb:
All streets in time are visited.

Then children strewn on steps or road,
Or women coming from the shops
Past smells of different dinners, see
A wild white face that overtops
Red stretcher-blankets momently
As it is carried in and stowed,

And sense the solving emptiness
That lies just under all we do,
And for a second get it whole,
So permanent and blank and true.
The fastened doors recede. *Poor soul,*
They whisper at their own distress;

For borne away in deadened air
May go the sudden shut of loss
Round something nearly at an end,
And what cohered in it across
The years, the unique random blend
Of families and fashions, there

At last begin to loosen. Far
From the exchange of love to lie
Unreachable inside a room
The traffic parts to let go by
Brings closer what is left to come,
And dulls to distance all we are.

10 January 1961 TWW

Naturally the Foundation will Bear Your Expenses

Hurrying to catch my Comet
    One dark November day,
Which soon would snatch me from it
    To the sunshine of Bombay,
I pondered pages Berkeley
    Not three weeks since had heard,
Perceiving Chatto darkly
    Through the mirror of the Third.

Crowds, colourless and careworn,
    Had made my taxi late,
Yet not till I was airborne
    Did I recall the date –
That day when Queen and Minister
    And Band of Guards and all
Still act their solemn-sinister
    Wreath-rubbish in Whitehall.

It used to make me throw up,
    These mawkish nursery games:
O when will England grow up?
    – But I outsoar the Thames,
And dwindle off down Auster
    To greet Professor Lal
(He once met Morgan Forster),
    My contact and my pal.

22 February 1961 TWW

[134]

The Large Cool Store

The large cool store selling cheap clothes
Set out in simple sizes plainly
(Knitwear, Summer Casuals, Hose,
In browns and greys, maroon and navy)
Conjures the weekday world of those

Who leave at dawn low terraced houses
Timed for factory, yard and site.
But past the heaps of shirts and trousers
Spread the stands of Modes For Night:
Machine-embroidered, thin as blouses,

Lemon, sapphire, moss-green, rose
Bri-Nylon Baby-Dolls and Shorties
Flounce in clusters. To suppose
They share that world, to think their sort is
Matched by something in it, shows

How separate and unearthly love is,
Or women are, or what they do,
Or in our young unreal wishes
Seem to be: synthetic, new,
And natureless in ecstasies.

18 June 1961 TWW

Here

Swerving east, from rich industrial shadows
And traffic all night north; swerving through fields
Too thin and thistled to be called meadows,
And now and then a harsh-named halt, that shields
Workmen at dawn; swerving to solitude
Of skies and scarecrows, haystacks, hares and pheasants,
And the widening river's slow presence,
The piled gold clouds, the shining gull-marked mud,

Gathers to the surprise of a large town:
Here domes and statues, spires and cranes cluster
Beside grain-scattered streets, barge-crowded water,
And residents from raw estates, brought down
The dead straight miles by stealing flat-faced trolleys,
Push through plate-glass swing doors to their desires –
Cheap suits, red kitchen-ware, sharp shoes, iced lollies,
Electric mixers, toasters, washers, driers –

A cut-price crowd, urban yet simple, dwelling
Where only salesmen and relations come
Within a terminate and fishy-smelling
Pastoral of ships up streets, the slave museum,
Tattoo-shops, consulates, grim head-scarfed wives;
And out beyond its mortgaged half-built edges
Fast-shadowed wheat-fields, running high as hedges,
Isolate villages, where removed lives

Loneliness clarifies. Here silence stands
Like heat. Here leaves unnoticed thicken,
Hidden weeds flower, neglected waters quicken,
Luminously-peopled air ascends;
And past the poppies bluish neutral distance

Ends the land suddenly beyond a beach
Of shapes and shingle. Here is unfenced existence:
Facing the sun, untalkative, out of reach.

8 October 1961 TWW

Nothing To Be Said

For nations vague as weed,
For nomads among stones,
Small-statured cross-faced tribes
And cobble-close families
In mill-towns on dark mornings
Life is slow dying.

So are their separate ways
Of building, benediction,
Measuring love and money
Ways of slow dying.
The day spent hunting pig
Or holding a garden-party,

Hours giving evidence
Or birth, advance
On death equally slowly.
And saying so to some
Means nothing; others it leaves
Nothing to be said.

18 October 1961 TWW

'And now the leaves suddenly lose strength'

And now the leaves suddenly lose strength.
Decaying towers stand still, lurid, lanes-long,
And seen from landing windows, or the length
Of gardens, rubricate afternoons. New strong
Rain-bearing night-winds come: then
Leaves chase warm buses, speckle statued air,
Pile up in corners, fetch out vague broomed men
Through mists at morning.
                          And no matter where goes down,
The sallow lapsing drift in fields
Or squares behind hoardings, all men hesitate
Separately, always, seeing another year gone –
Frockcoated gentleman, farmer at his gate,
Villein with mattock, soldiers on their shields,
All silent, watching the winter coming on.

3 November 1961

Broadcast

Giant whispering and coughing from
Vast Sunday-full and organ-frowned-on spaces
Precede a sudden scuttle on the drum,
'The Queen', and huge resettling. Then begins
A snivel on the violins:
I think of your face among all those faces,

Beautiful and devout before
Cascades of monumental slithering,
One of your gloves unnoticed on the floor
Beside those new, slightly-outmoded shoes.
Here it goes quickly dark. I lose
All but the outline of the still and withering

Leaves on half-emptied trees. Behind
The glowing wavebands, rabid storms of chording
By being distant overpower my mind
All the more shamelessly, their cut-off shout
Leaving me desperate to pick out
Your hands, tiny in all that air, applauding.

6 *November 1961* TWW

Breadfruit

Boys dream of native girls who bring breadfruit,
        Whatever they are,
As brides to teach them how to execute
Sixteen sexual positions on the sand;
This makes them join (the boys) the tennis club,
Jive at the Mecca, use deodorants, and
On Saturdays squire ex-schoolgirls to the pub
        By private car.

Such uncorrected visions end in church
        Or registrar:
A mortgaged semi- with a silver birch;
Nippers; the widowed mum; having to scheme
With money; illness; age. So absolute
Maturity falls, when old men sit and dream
Of naked native girls who bring breadfruit
        Whatever they are.

19 November 1961 Critical Quarterly, Winter 1961

'A slight relax of air where cold was'

A slight relax of air where cold was
And water trickles; dark ruinous light,
Scratched like old film, above wet slates withdraws.
At garden-ends, on railway banks, sad white
Shrinkage of snow shows cleaner than the net
Stiffened like ectoplasm in front windows.

Shielded, what sorts of life are stirring yet:
Legs lagged like drains, slippers soft as fungus,
The gas and grate, the old cold sour grey bed.
Some ajar face, corpse-stubbled, bends round
To see the sky over the aerials –
Sky, absent paleness across which the gulls
Wing to the Corporation rubbish ground.
A slight relax of air. All is not dead.

13 January 1962

Wild Oats

About twenty years ago
Two girls came in where I worked –
A bosomy English rose
And her friend in specs I could talk to.
Faces in those days sparked
The whole shooting-match off, and I doubt
If ever one had like hers:
But it was the friend I took out,

And in seven years after that
Wrote over four hundred letters,
Gave a ten-guinea ring
I got back in the end, and met
At numerous cathedral cities
Unknown to the clergy. I believe
I met beautiful twice. She was trying
Both times (so I thought) not to laugh.

Parting, after about five
Rehearsals, was an agreement
That I was too selfish, withdrawn,
And easily bored to love.
Well, useful to get that learnt.
In my wallet are still two snaps
Of bosomy rose with fur gloves on.
Unlucky charms, perhaps.

12 *May* 1962 TWW

Essential Beauty

In frames as large as rooms that face all ways
And block the ends of streets with giant loaves,
Screen graves with custard, cover slums with praise
Of motor-oil and cuts of salmon, shine
Perpetually these sharply-pictured groves
Of how life should be. High above the gutter
A silver knife sinks into golden butter,
A glass of milk stands in a meadow, and
Well-balanced families, in fine
Midsummer weather, owe their smiles, their cars,
Even their youth, to that small cube each hand
Stretches towards. These, and the deep armchairs
Aligned to cups at bedtime, radiant bars
(Gas or electric), quarter-profile cats
By slippers on warm mats,
Reflect none of the rained-on streets and squares

They dominate outdoors. Rather, they rise
Serenely to proclaim pure crust, pure foam,
Pure coldness to our live imperfect eyes
That stare beyond this world, where nothing's made
As new or washed quite clean, seeking the home
All such inhabit. There, dark raftered pubs
Are filled with white-clothed ones from tennis-clubs,
And the boy puking his heart out in the Gents
Just missed them, as the pensioner paid
A halfpenny more for Granny Graveclothes' Tea
To taste old age, and dying smokers sense
Walking towards them through some dappled park
As if on water that unfocused she

No match lit up, nor drag ever brought near,
Who now stands newly clear,
Smiling, and recognising, and going dark.

26 June 1962 TWW

Send No Money

Standing under the fobbed
Impendent belly of Time
Tell me the truth, I said,
Teach me the way things go.
All the other lads there
Were itching to have a bash,
But I thought wanting unfair:
It and finding out clash.

So he patted my head, booming *Boy,*
There's no green in your eye:
Sit here, and watch the hail
Of occurrence clobber life out
To a shape no one sees –
Dare you look at that straight?
Oh thank you, I said, *Oh yes please,*
And sat down to wait.

Half life is over now,
And I meet full face on dark mornings
The bestial visor, bent in
By the blows of what happened to happen.
What does it prove? Sod all.
In this way I spent youth,
Tracing the trite untransferable
Truss-advertisement, truth.

21 August 1962 TWW

Toads Revisited

Walking around in the park
Should feel better than work:
The lake, the sunshine,
The grass to lie on,

Blurred playground noises
Beyond black-stockinged nurses –
Not a bad place to be.
Yet it doesn't suit me,

Being one of the men
You meet of an afternoon:
Palsied old step-takers,
Hare-eyed clerks with the jitters,

Waxed-fleshed out-patients
Still vague from accidents,
And characters in long coats
Deep in the litter-baskets –

All dodging the toad work
By being stupid or weak.
Think of being them!
Hearing the hours chime,

Watching the bread delivered,
The sun by clouds covered,
The children going home;
Think of being them,

Turning over their failures
By some bed of lobelias,
Nowhere to go but indoors,
No friends but empty chairs –

No, give me my in-tray,
My loaf-haired secretary,
My shall-I-keep-the-call-in-Sir:
What else can I answer,

When the lights come on at four
At the end of another year?
Give me your arm, old toad;
Help me down Cemetery Road.

October 1962 TWW

Sunny Prestatyn

Come To Sunny Prestatyn
Laughed the girl on the poster,
Kneeling up on the sand
In tautened white satin.
Behind her, a hunk of coast, a
Hotel with palms
Seemed to expand from her thighs and
Spread breast-lifting arms.

She was slapped up one day in March.
A couple of weeks, and her face
Was snaggle-toothed and boss-eyed;
Huge tits and a fissured crotch
Were scored well in, and the space
Between her legs held scrawls
That set her fairly astride
A tuberous cock and balls

Autographed *Titch Thomas*, while
Someone had used a knife
Or something to stab right through
The moustached lips of her smile.
She was too good for this life.
Very soon, a great transverse tear
Left only a hand and some blue.
Now *Fight Cancer* is there.

October ? 1962 TWW

Love

The difficult part of love
Is being selfish enough,
Is having the blind persistence
To upset an existence
Just for your own sake.
What cheek it must take.

And then the unselfish side –
How can you be satisfied,
Putting someone else first
So that you come off worst?
My life is for me.
As well ignore gravity.

Still, vicious or virtuous,
Love suits most of us.
Only the bleeder found
Selfish this wrong way round
Is ever wholly rebuffed,
And he can get stuffed.

7 December 1962 Critical Quarterly,
Summer 1966

Long Last

Suddenly, not long before
Her eighty-first birthday,
The younger sister died.
Next morning, the elder lay
Asking the open door
Why it was light outside,

Since nobody had put on
The kettle, or raked the ashes,
Or come to help her find
The dark way through her dress.
This went on till nearly one.
Later, she hid behind

The gas stove. 'Amy's gone,
Isn't she,' they remember her saying,
And 'No' when the married niece
Told her the van was coming.
Her neck was leaf-brown.
She left cake on the mantelpiece.

This long last childhood
Nothing provides for.
What can it do each day
But hunt that imminent door
Through which all that understood
Has hidden away?

3 February 1963

Dockery and Son

'Dockery was junior to you,
Wasn't he?' said the Dean. 'His son's here now.'
Death-suited, visitant, I nod. 'And do
You keep in touch with—' Or remember how
Black-gowned, unbreakfasted, and still half-tight
We used to stand before that desk, to give
'Our version' of 'these incidents last night'?
I try the door of where I used to live:

Locked. The lawn spreads dazzlingly wide.
A known bell chimes. I catch my train, ignored.
Canal and clouds and colleges subside
Slowly from view. But Dockery, good Lord,
Anyone up today must have been born
In '43, when I was twenty-one.
If he was younger, did he get this son
At nineteen, twenty? Was he that withdrawn

High-collared public-schoolboy, sharing rooms
With Cartwright who was killed? Well, it just shows
How much . . . How little . . . Yawning, I suppose
I fell asleep, waking at the fumes
And furnace-glares of Sheffield, where I changed,
And ate an awful pie, and walked along
The platform to its end to see the ranged
Joining and parting lines reflect a strong

Unhindered moon. To have no son, no wife,
No house or land still seemed quite natural.
Only a numbness registered the shock
Of finding out how much had gone of life,
How widely from the others. Dockery, now:
Only nineteen, he must have taken stock

Of what he wanted, and been capable
Of . . . No, that's not the difference: rather, how

Convinced he was he should be added to!
Why did he think adding meant increase?
To me it was dilution. Where do these
Innate assumptions come from? Not from what
We think truest, or most want to do:
Those warp tight-shut, like doors. They're more a style
Our lives bring with them: habit for a while,
Suddenly they harden into all we've got

And how we got it; looked back on, they rear
Like sand-clouds, thick and close, embodying
For Dockery a son, for me nothing,
Nothing with all a son's harsh patronage.
Life is first boredom, then fear.
Whether or not we use it, it goes,
And leaves what something hidden from us chose,
And age, and then the only end of age.

28 March 1963 TWW

The Dance

'Drink, sex and jazz – all sweet things, brother: far
Too sweet to be diluted to "a dance",
That muddled middle-class pretence at each
No one who really . . . ' But contemptuous speech
Fades at my equally-contemptuous glance,
That in the darkening mirror sees
The shame of evening trousers, evening tie.
White candles stir within the chestnut trees.
The sun is low. The pavements are half-dry.
Cigarettes, matches, keys –
All this, simply to be where you are.

Half willing, half abandoning the will,
I let myself by specious steps be haled
Across the wide circumference of my scorn.
No escape now. Large cars parked round the lawn
Scan my approach. The light has almost failed,
And the faint thudding stridency
Some band we have been 'fortunate to secure'
Proclaims from lit-up windows comes to me
More as a final warning than a lure:
Alien territory . . .
And once I gain the upstairs hall, that's still

Our same familiar barn ballooned and chained,
The floor reverberates as with alarm:
Not you, not here. I edge along the noise
Towards a trestled bar, lacking the poise
To look about me; served, maturer calm
Permits a leaning-back, to view
The whole harmoniously-shifting crowd,
And with some people at some table, you.
Why gulp? The scene is normal and allowed:

Professional colleagues do
Assemble socially, are entertained

By sitting dressed like this, in rooms like these,
Saying I can't guess what – just fancy, when
They could be really drinking, or in bed,
Or listening to records – so, instead
Of waiting till you look my way, and then
Grinning my hopes, I stalk your chair
Beside the deafening band, where raised faces
Sag into silence at my standing there,
And your eyes greet me over commonplaces,
And your arms are bare,
And I wish desperately for qualities

Moments like this demand, and which I lack.
I face you on the floor, clumsily, as
Something starts up. Your look is challenging
And not especially friendly: everything
I look to for protection – the mock jazz,
The gilt-edged Founder, through the door
The 'running buffet supper' – grows less real.
Suddenly it strikes me you are acting more
Than ever you would put in words; I feel
The impact, open, raw,
Of a tremendous answer banging back

As if I'd asked a question. In the slug
And snarl of music, under cover of
A few permitted movements, you suggest
A whole consenting language, that my chest
Quickens and tightens at, descrying love –
Something acutely local, me
As I am now, and you as you are now,
And now; something acutely transitory
The slightest impulse could deflect to how

[155]

We act eternally.
Why not snatch it? Your fingers tighten, tug,

Then slacken altogether. I am caught
By some shoptalking shit who leads me off
To supper and his bearded wife, to stand
Bemused and coffee-holding while the band
Restarts off-stage, and they in tempo scoff
Small things I couldn't look at, rent
By wondering who has got you now, and whether
That serious restlessness was what you meant,
Or was it all those things mixed up together?
(Drink, sex and jazz.) Content
To let it seem I've just been taken short,

I eel back to the bar, where they're surprised
That anyone still wants to drink, and find
You and a weed from Plant Psychology
Loose to the music. So you looked at me,
As if about to whistle; so outlined
Sharp sensual truisms, so yearned –
I breathe in, deeply. It's pathetic how
So much most people half my age have learned
Consumes me only as I watch you now,
The tense elation turned
To something snapped off short, and localised

Half-way between the gullet and the tongue.
The evening falters. Couples in their coats
Are leaving gaps already, and the rest
Move tables closer. I lean forward, lest
I go on seeing you, and souse my throat's
Imminent block with gin. How right
I should have been to keep away, and let
You have your innocent-guilty-innocent night
Of switching partners in your own sad set:

How useless to invite
The sickened breathlessness of being young

Into my life again! I ought to go,
If going would do any good; instead,
I let the barman tell me how it was
Before the war, when there were sheep and grass
In place of Social Pathics; then I tread
Heavily to the Gents, and see
My coat patiently hanging, and the chains
And taps and basins that would also be
There when the sheep were. Chuckles from the drains
Decide me suddenly:
Ring for a car right now. But doing so

Needs pennies, and in making for the bar
For change I see your lot are waving, till
I have to cross and smile and stay and share
Instead of walking out, and so from there
The evening starts again; its first dark chill
And omen-laden music seem
No more than rain round a conservatory
Oafishly warm inside. I sit and beam
At everyone, even the weed, and he
Unfolds some crazy scheme
He's got for making wine from beetroot, far

Too incoherent to survive the band;
Then there's a *Which*-fed argument – but why
Enumerate? For now we take the floor
Quite unremarked-on, and I feel once more
That silent beckoning from you verify
All I remember – weaker, but
Something in me starts toppling. I can sense
By staring at your eyes (hazel, half-shut)

Endless receding Saturdays, their dense
And spot-light-fingered glut
Of never-resting hair-dos; understand

30 June 1963–12 May 1964 (unfinished)

Solar

Suspended lion face
Spilling at the centre
Of an unfurnished sky
How still you stand,
And how unaided
Single stalkless flower
You pour unrecompensed.

The eye sees you
Simplified by distance
Into an origin,
Your petalled head of flames
Continuously exploding.
Heat is the echo of your
Gold.

Coined there among
Lonely horizontals
You exist openly.
Our needs hourly
Climb and return like angels.
Unclosing like a hand,
You give for ever.

4 November 1964 HW

Ape Experiment Room

Buried among white rooms
Whose lights in clusters beam
Like suddenly-caused pain,
And where behind rows of mesh
Uneasy shifting resumes
As sterilisers steam
And the routine begins again
Of putting questions to flesh

That no one would think to ask
But a Ph.D. with a beard
And nympho wife who –

                              But
There, I was saying, are found
The bushy, T-shaped mask,
And below, the smaller, eared
Head like a grave nut,
And the arms folded round.

24 February 1965

Administration

Day by day your estimation clocks up
Who deserves a smile and who a frown,
And girls you have to tell to pull their socks up
Are those whose pants you'd most like to pull down.

3 March 1965

How Distant

How distant, the departure of young men
Down valleys, or watching
The green shore past the salt-white cordage
Rising and falling,

Cattlemen, or carpenters, or keen
Simply to get away
From married villages before morning,
Melodeons play

On tiny decks past fraying cliffs of water
Or late at night
Sweet under the differently-swung stars,
When the chance sight

Of a girl doing her laundry in the steerage
Ramifies endlessly.
This is being young,
Assumption of the startled century

Like new store clothes,
The huge decisions printed out by feet
Inventing where they tread,
The random windows conjuring a street.

24 November 1965 HW

Friday Night in the Royal Station Hotel

Light spreads darkly downwards from the high
Clusters of lights over empty chairs
That face each other, coloured differently.
Through open doors, the dining-room declares
A larger loneliness of knives and glass
And silence laid like carpet. A porter reads
An unsold evening paper. Hours pass,
And all the salesmen have gone back to Leeds,
Leaving full ashtrays in the Conference Room.

In shoeless corridors, the lights burn. How
Isolated, like a fort, it is –
The headed paper, made for writing home
(If home existed) letters of exile: *Now
Night comes on. Waves fold behind villages.*

20 *May* 1966 HW

[163]

'Scratch on the scratch pad'

Scratch on the scratch pad
Rabbit *memoranda* –
Handkerchiefs and horoscopes,
Holland gowns and grander;
Scratch on the scratch pad
Rabbit *memorabilia* –
Spectacles and spirit lamps,
Steeple hats and sillier;
Much we buy each market day,
More still obtain:
All, all is carried home
By slow evening train.

19 July 1966 (unfinished?)

High Windows

When I see a couple of kids
And guess he's fucking her and she's
Taking pills or wearing a diaphragm,
I know this is paradise

Everyone old has dreamed of all their lives –
Bonds and gestures pushed to one side
Like an outdated combine harvester,
And everyone young going down the long slide

To happiness, endlessly. I wonder if
Anyone looked at me, forty years back,
And thought, *That'll be the life;*
No God any more, or sweating in the dark

About hell and that, or having to hide
What you think of the priest. He
And his lot will all go down the long slide
Like free bloody birds. And immediately

Rather than words comes the thought of high windows:
The sun-comprehending glass,
And beyond it, the deep blue air, that shows
Nothing, and is nowhere, and is endless.

12 February 1967 HW

The Trees

The trees are coming into leaf
Like something almost being said;
The recent buds relax and spread,
Their greenness is a kind of grief.

Is it that they are born again
And we grow old? No, they die too.
Their yearly trick of looking new
Is written down in rings of grain.

Yet still the unresting castles thresh
In fullgrown thickness every May.
Last year is dead, they seem to say,
Begin afresh, afresh, afresh.

2 June 1967 HW

Annus Mirabilis

Sexual intercourse began
In nineteen sixty-three
(Which was rather late for me) –
Between the end of the *Chatterley* ban
And the Beatles' first LP.

Up till then there'd only been
A sort of bargaining,
A wrangle for a ring,
A shame that started at sixteen
And spread to everything.

Then all at once the quarrel sank:
Everyone felt the same,
And every life became
A brilliant breaking of the bank,
A quite unlosable game.

So life was never better than
In nineteen sixty-three
(Though just too late for me) –
Between the end of the *Chatterley* ban
And the Beatles' first LP.

16 June 1967 HW

Sympathy in White Major

When I drop four cubes of ice
Chimingly in a glass, and add
Three goes of gin, a lemon slice,
And let a ten-ounce tonic void
In foaming gulps until it smothers
Everything else up to the edge,
I lift the lot in private pledge:
He devoted his life to others.

While other people wore like clothes
The human beings in their days
I set myself to bring to those
Who thought I could the lost displays;
It didn't work for them or me,
But all concerned were nearer thus
(Or so we thought) to all the fuss
Than if we'd missed it separately.

A decent chap, a real good sort,
Straight as a die, one of the best,
A brick, a trump, a proper sport,
Head and shoulders above the rest;
How many lives would have been duller
Had he not been here below?
Here's to the whitest man I know –
Though white is not my favourite colour.

31 August 1967 HW

Sad Steps

Groping back to bed after a piss
I part thick curtains, and am startled by
The rapid clouds, the moon's cleanliness.

Four o'clock: wedge-shadowed gardens lie
Under a cavernous, a wind-picked sky.
There's something laughable about this,

The way the moon dashes through clouds that blow
Loosely as cannon-smoke to stand apart
(Stone-coloured light sharpening the roofs below)

High and preposterous and separate –
Lozenge of love! Medallion of art!
O wolves of memory! Immensements! No,

One shivers slightly, looking up there.
The hardness and the brightness and the plain
Far-reaching singleness of that wide stare

Is a reminder of the strength and pain
Of being young; that it can't come again,
But is for others undiminished somewhere.

24 April 1968 HW

Posterity

Jake Balokowsky, my biographer,
Has this page microfilmed. Sitting inside
His air-conditioned cell at Kennedy
In jeans and sneakers, he's no call to hide
Some slight impatience with his destiny:
'I'm stuck with this old fart at least a year;

I wanted to teach school in Tel Aviv,
But Myra's folks' – he makes the money sign –
'Insisted I got tenure. When there's kids –'
He shrugs. 'It's stinking dead, the research line;
Just let me put this bastard on the skids,
I'll get a couple of semesters leave

To work on Protest Theater.' They both rise,
Make for the Coke dispenser. 'What's he like?
Christ, I just told you. Oh, you know the thing,
That crummy textbook stuff from Freshman Psych,
Not out of kicks or something happening –
One of those old-type *natural* fouled-up guys.'

17 June 1968 HW

Homage to a Government

Next year we are to bring the soldiers home
For lack of money, and it is all right.
Places they guarded, or kept orderly,
Must guard themselves, and keep themselves orderly.
We want the money for ourselves at home
Instead of working. And this is all right.

It's hard to say who wanted it to happen,
But now it's been decided nobody minds.
The places are a long way off, not here,
Which is all right, and from what we hear
The soldiers there only made trouble happen.
Next year we shall be easier in our minds.

Next year we shall be living in a country
That brought its soldiers home for lack of money.
The statues will be standing in the same
Tree-muffled squares, and look nearly the same.
Our children will not know it's a different country.
All we can hope to leave them now is money.

10 January 1969 HW

'When the Russian tanks roll westward'

When the Russian tanks roll westward, what defence for you
and me?
Colonel Sloman's Essex Rifles? The Light Horse of L.S.E.?

March ? 1969 'Black Paper two: the Crisis in Education', 1969

To the Sea

To step over the low wall that divides
Road from concrete walk above the shore
Brings sharply back something known long before –
The miniature gaiety of seasides.
Everything crowds under the low horizon:
Steep beach, blue water, towels, red bathing caps,
The small hushed waves' repeated fresh collapse
Up the warm yellow sand, and further off
A white steamer stuck in the afternoon –

Still going on, all of it, still going on!
To lie, eat, sleep in hearing of the surf
(Ears to transistors, that sound tame enough
Under the sky), or gently up and down
Lead the uncertain children, frilled in white
And grasping at enormous air, or wheel
The rigid old along for them to feel
A final summer, plainly still occurs
As half an annual pleasure, half a rite,

As when, happy at being on my own,
I searched the sand for Famous Cricketers,
Or, farther back, my parents, listeners
To the same seaside quack, first became known.
Strange to it now, I watch the cloudless scene:
The same clear water over smoothed pebbles,
The distant bathers' weak protesting trebles
Down at its edge, and then the cheap cigars,
The chocolate-papers, tea-leaves, and, between

The rocks, the rusting soup-tins, till the first
Few families start the trek back to the cars.
The white steamer has gone. Like breathed-on glass
The sunlight has turned milky. If the worst

Of flawless weather is our falling short,
It may be that through habit these do best,
Coming to water clumsily undressed
Yearly; teaching their children by a sort
Of clowning; helping the old, too, as they ought.

October 1969 HW

The Explosion

On the day of the explosion
Shadows pointed towards the pithead:
In the sun the slagheap slept.

Down the lane came men in pitboots
Coughing oath-edged talk and pipe-smoke,
Shouldering off the freshened silence.

One chased after rabbits; lost them;
Came back with a nest of lark's eggs;
Showed them; lodged them in the grasses.

So they passed in beards and moleskins,
Fathers, brothers, nicknames, laughter,
Through the tall gates standing open.

At noon, there came a tremor; cows
Stopped chewing for a second; sun,
Scarfed as in a heat-haze, dimmed.

The dead go on before us, they
Are sitting in God's house in comfort,
We shall see them face to face –

Plain as lettering in the chapels
It was said, and for a second
Wives saw men of the explosion

Larger than in life they managed –
Gold as on a coin, or walking
Somehow from the sun towards them,

One showing the eggs unbroken.

5 January 1970 HW

How

How high they build hospitals!
Lighted cliffs, against dawns
Of days people will die on.
I can see one from here.

How cold winter keeps
And long, ignoring
Our need now for kindness.
Spring has got into the wrong year.

How few people are,
Held apart by acres
Of housing, and children
With their shallow violent eyes.

10 April 1970 Wave, Autumn 1970

The Card-Players

Jan van Hogspeuw staggers to the door
And pisses at the dark. Outside, the rain
Courses in cart-ruts down the deep mud lane.
Inside, Dirk Dogstoerd pours himself some more,
And holds a cinder to his clay with tongs,
Belching out smoke. Old Prijck snores with the gale,
His skull face firelit; someone behind drinks ale,
And opens mussels, and croaks scraps of songs
Towards the ham-hung rafters about love.
Dirk deals the cards. Wet century-wide trees
Clash in surrounding starlessness above
This lamplit cave, where Jan turns back and farts,
Gobs at the grate, and hits the queen of hearts.

Rain, wind and fire! The secret, bestial peace!

6 May 1970 HW

Dublinesque

Down stucco sidestreets,
Where light is pewter
And afternoon mist
Brings lights on in shops
Above race-guides and rosaries,
A funeral passes.

The hearse is ahead,
But after there follows
A troop of streetwalkers
In wide flowered hats,
Leg-of-mutton sleeves,
And ankle-length dresses.

There is an air of great friendliness,
As if they were honouring
One they were fond of;
Some caper a few steps,
Skirts held skilfully
(Someone claps time),

And of great sadness also.
As they wend away
A voice is heard singing
Of Kitty, or Katy,
As if the name meant once
All love, all beauty.

6 June 1970 HW

Poem about Oxford
for Monica

City we shared without knowing
In blacked-out and butterless days,
Till we left, and were glad to be going
(Unlike the arselicker who stays),
Does it stick in our minds as a touchstone
Of learning and *la politesse*?
For while the old place hadn't much tone,
Two others we know have got less.

Perhaps not. And yet so much is certain:
Aside from more durable things,
I'm glad you don't say you're from Girton,
You'd sooner I wasn't at King's;
To all that it meant – a full notecase,
Dull Bodley, draught beer, and dark blue,
And most often losing the Boat Race –
You're added, as I am for you.

So thirty years on, when the cake-queues
And coffees have gone by the board,
And new men in new labs make break-throughs,
Old buildings are cleaned and restored,
And students live up to what's said about
Their like in Black Papers and more,
It holds us, like that *Fleae* we read about
In the depths of the Second World War.

1970?

[179]

This Be The Verse

They fuck you up, your mum and dad.
   They may not mean to, but they do.
They fill you with the faults they had
   And add some extra, just for you.

But they were fucked up in their turn
   By fools in old-style hats and coats,
Who half the time were soppy-stern
   And half at one another's throats.

Man hands on misery to man.
   It deepens like a coastal shelf.
Get out as early as you can,
   And don't have any kids yourself.

April ? 1971 HW

Vers de Société

My wife and I have asked a crowd of craps
To come and waste their time and ours: perhaps
You'd care to join us? In a pig's arse, friend.
Day comes to an end.
The gas fire breathes, the trees are darkly swayed.
And so *Dear Warlock-Williams: I'm afraid* –

Funny how hard it is to be alone.
I could spend half my evenings, if I wanted,
Holding a glass of washing sherry, canted
Over to catch the drivel of some bitch
Who's read nothing but *Which*;
Just think of all the spare time that has flown

Straight into nothingness by being filled
With forks and faces, rather than repaid
Under a lamp, hearing the noise of wind,
And looking out to see the moon thinned
To an air-sharpened blade.
A life, and yet how sternly it's instilled

All solitude is selfish. No one now
Believes the hermit with his gown and dish
Talking to God (who's gone too); the big wish
Is to have people nice to you, which means
Doing it back somehow.
Virtue is social. Are, then, these routines

Playing at goodness, like going to church?
Something that bores us, something we don't do well
(Asking that ass about his fool research)
But try to feel, because, however crudely,
It shows us what should be?
Too subtle, that. Too decent, too. Oh hell,

Only the young can be alone freely.
The time is shorter now for company,
And sitting by a lamp more often brings
Not peace, but other things.
Beyond the light stand failure and remorse
Whispering *Dear Warlock-Williams: Why, of course* –

19 May 1971 HW

Cut Grass

Cut grass lies frail:
Brief is the breath
Mown stalks exhale.
Long, long the death

It dies in the white hours
Of young-leafed June
With chestnut flowers,
With hedges snowlike strewn,

White lilac bowed,
Lost lanes of Queen Anne's lace,
And that high-builded cloud
Moving at summer's pace.

3 June 1971 HW

Forget What Did

Stopping the diary
Was a stun to memory,
Was a blank starting,

One no longer cicatrized
By such words, such actions
As bleakened waking.

I wanted them over,
Hurried to burial
And looked back on

Like the wars and winters
Missing behind the windows
Of an opaque childhood.

And the empty pages?
Should they ever be filled
Let it be with observed

Celestial recurrences,
The day the flowers come,
And when the birds go.

6 August 1971 HW

'I have started to say'

I have started to say
'A quarter of a century'
Or 'thirty years back'
About my own life.

It makes me breathless.
It's like falling and recovering
In huge gesturing loops
Through an empty sky.

All that's left to happen
Is some deaths (my own included).
Their order, and their manner,
Remain to be learnt.

October 1971

Livings

I

I deal with farmers, things like dips and feed.
Every third month I book myself in at
The —— Hotel in —ton for three days.
The boots carries my lean old leather case
Up to a single, where I hang my hat.
One beer, and then 'the dinner', at which I read
The —*shire Times* from soup to stewed pears.
Births, deaths. For sale. Police court. Motor spares.

Afterwards, whisky in the Smoke Room: Clough,
Margetts, the Captain, Dr. Watterson;
Who makes ends meet, who's taking the knock,
Government tariffs, wages, price of stock.
Smoke hangs under the light. The pictures on
The walls are comic – hunting, the trenches, stuff
Nobody minds or notices. A sound
Of dominoes from the Bar. I stand a round.

Later, the square is empty: a big sky
Drains down the estuary like the bed
Of a gold river, and the Customs House
Still has its office lit. I drowse
Between ex-Army sheets, wondering why
I think it's worth while coming. Father's dead:
He used to, but the business now is mine.
It's time for change, in nineteen twenty-nine.

16 October 1971 HW

[186]

Seventy feet down
The sea explodes upwards,
Relapsing, to slaver
Off landing-stage steps –
Running suds, rejoice!

Rocks writhe back to sight.
Mussels, limpets,
Husband their tenacity
In the freezing slither –
Creatures, I cherish you!

By day, sky builds
Grape-dark over the salt
Unsown stirring fields.
Radio rubs its legs,
Telling me of elsewhere:

Barometers falling,
Ports wind-shuttered,
Fleets pent like hounds,
Fires in humped inns
Kippering sea-pictures –

Keep it all off!
By night, snow swerves
(O loose moth world)
Through the stare travelling
Leather-black waters.

Guarded by brilliance
I set plate and spoon,
And after, divining-cards.
Lit shelved liners
Grope like mad worlds westward.

23 November 1971 HW

III

Tonight we dine without the Master
(Nocturnal vapours do not please);
The port goes round so much the faster,
Topics are raised with no less ease –
Which advowson looks the fairest,
What the wood from Snape will fetch,
Names for *pudendum mulieris*,
Why is Judas like Jack Ketch?

The candleflames grow thin, then broaden:
Our butler Starveling piles the logs
And sets behind the screen a jordan
(Quicker than going to the bogs).
The wine heats temper and complexion:
Oath-enforced assertions fly
On rheumy fevers, resurrection,
Regicide and rabbit pie.

The fields around are cold and muddy,
The cobbled streets close by are still,
A sizar shivers at his study,
The kitchen cat has made a kill;
The bells discuss the hour's gradations,
Dusty shelves hold prayers and proofs:
Above, Chaldean constellations
Sparkle over crowded roofs.

10 December 1971 HW

Going, Going

I thought it would last my time –
The sense that, beyond the town,
There would always be fields and farms,
Where the village louts could climb
Such trees as were not cut down;
I knew there'd be false alarms

In the papers about old streets
And split-level shopping, but some
Have always been left so far;
And when the old part retreats
As the bleak high-risers come
We can always escape in the car.

Things are tougher than we are, just
As earth will always respond
However we mess it about;
Chuck filth in the sea, if you must:
The tides will be clean beyond.
– But what do I feel now? Doubt?

Or age, simply? The crowd
Is young in the Mı café;
Their kids are screaming for more –
More houses, more parking allowed,
More caravan sites, more pay.
On the Business Page, a score

Of spectacled grins approve
Some takeover bid that entails
Five per cent profit (and ten
Per cent more in the estuaries): move
Your works to the unspoilt dales
(Grey area grants)! And when

You try to get near the sea
In summer . . .
                    It seems, just now,
To be happening so very fast;
Despite all the land left free
For the first time I feel somehow
That it isn't going to last,

That before I snuff it, the whole
Boiling will be bricked in
Except for the tourist parts –
First slum of Europe: a role
It won't be so hard to win,
With a cast of crooks and tarts.

And that will be England gone,
The shadows, the meadows, the lanes,
The guildhalls, the carved choirs.
There'll be books; it will linger on
In galleries; but all that remains
For us will be concrete and tyres.

Most things are never meant.
This won't be, most likely: but greeds
And garbage are too thick-strewn
To be swept up now, or invent
Excuses that make them all needs.
I just think it will happen, soon.

25 *January 1972* HW

The Building

Higher than the handsomest hotel
The lucent comb shows up for miles, but see,
All round it close-ribbed streets rise and fall
Like a great sigh out of the last century.
The porters are scruffy; what keep drawing up
At the entrance are not taxis; and in the hall
As well as creepers hangs a frightening smell.

There are paperbacks, and tea at so much a cup,
Like an airport lounge, but those who tamely sit
On rows of steel chairs turning the ripped mags
Haven't come far. More like a local bus,
These outdoor clothes and half-filled shopping bags
And faces restless and resigned, although
Every few minutes comes a kind of nurse

To fetch someone away: the rest refit
Cups back to saucers, cough, or glance below
Seats for dropped gloves or cards. Humans, caught
On ground curiously neutral, homes and names
Suddenly in abeyance; some are young,
Some old, but most at that vague age that claims
The end of choice, the last of hope; and all

Here to confess that something has gone wrong.
It must be error of a serious sort,
For see how many floors it needs, how tall
It's grown by now, and how much money goes
In trying to correct it. See the time,
Half-past eleven on a working day,
And these picked out of it; see, as they climb

To their appointed levels, how their eyes
Go to each other, guessing; on the way

Someone's wheeled past, in washed-to-rags ward clothes:
They see him, too. They're quiet. To realise
This new thing held in common makes them quiet,
For past these doors are rooms, and rooms past those,
And more rooms yet, each one further off

And harder to return from; and who knows
Which he will see, and when? For the moment, wait,
Look down at the yard. Outside seems old enough:
Red brick, lagged pipes, and someone walking by it
Out to the car park, free. Then, past the gate,
Traffic; a locked church; short terraced streets
Where kids chalk games, and girls with hair-dos fetch

Their separates from the cleaners – O world,
Your loves, your chances, are beyond the stretch
Of any hand from here! And so, unreal,
A touching dream to which we all are lulled
But wake from separately. In it, conceits
And self-protecting ignorance congeal
To carry life, collapsing only when

Called to these corridors (for now once more
The nurse beckons –). Each gets up and goes
At last. Some will be out by lunch, or four;
Others, not knowing it, have come to join
The unseen congregations whose white rows
Lie set apart above – women, men;
Old, young; crude facets of the only coin

This place accepts. All know they are going to die.
Not yet, perhaps not here, but in the end,
And somewhere like this. That is what it means,
This clean-sliced cliff; a struggle to transcend

The thought of dying, for unless its powers
Outbuild cathedrals nothing contravenes
The coming dark, though crowds each evening try

With wasteful, weak, propitiatory flowers.

9 February 1972 HW

Heads in the Women's Ward

On pillow after pillow lies
The wild white hair and staring eyes;
Jaws stand open; necks are stretched
With every tendon sharply sketched;
A bearded mouth talks silently
To someone no one else can see.

Sixty years ago they smiled
At lover, husband, first-born child.

Smiles are for youth. For old age come
Death's terror and delirium.

6 March 1972 New Humanist, May 1972

The View

The view is fine from fifty,
  Experienced climbers say;
So, overweight and shifty,
  I turn to face the way
  That led me to this day.

Instead of fields and snowcaps
  And flowered lanes that twist,
The track breaks at my toe-caps
  And drops away in mist.
  The view does not exist.

Where has it gone, the lifetime?
  Search me. What's left is drear.
Unchilded and unwifed, I'm
  Able to view that clear:
  So final. And so near.

August ? 1972

The Old Fools

What do they think has happened, the old fools,
To make them like this? Do they somehow suppose
It's more grown-up when your mouth hangs open and drools,
And you keep on pissing yourself, and can't remember
Who called this morning? Or that, if they only chose,
They could alter things back to when they danced all night,
Or went to their wedding, or sloped arms some September?
Or do they fancy there's really been no change,
And they've always behaved as if they were crippled or tight,
Or sat through days of thin continuous dreaming
Watching light move? If they don't (and they can't), it's strange:
              Why aren't they screaming?

At death, you break up: the bits that were you
Start speeding away from each other for ever
With no one to see. It's only oblivion, true:
We had it before, but then it was going to end,
And was all the time merging with a unique endeavour
To bring to bloom the million-petalled flower
Of being here. Next time you can't pretend
There'll be anything else. And these are the first signs:
Not knowing how, not hearing who, the power
Of choosing gone. Their looks show that they're for it:
Ash hair, toad hands, prune face dried into lines –
              How can they ignore it?

Perhaps being old is having lighted rooms
Inside your head, and people in them, acting.
People you know, yet can't quite name; each looms
Like a deep loss restored, from known doors turning,
Setting down a lamp, smiling from a stair, extracting
A known book from the shelves; or sometimes only
The rooms themselves, chairs and a fire burning,
The blown bush at the window, or the sun's

Faint friendliness on the wall some lonely
Rain-ceased midsummer evening. That is where they live:
Not here and now, but where all happened once.
                    This is why they give

An air of baffled absence, trying to be there
Yet being here. For the rooms grow farther, leaving
Incompetent cold, the constant wear and tear
Of taken breath, and them crouching below
Extinction's alp, the old fools, never perceiving
How near it is. This must be what keeps them quiet:
The peak that stays in view wherever we go
For them is rising ground. Can they never tell
What is dragging them back, and how it will end ? Not at night?
Not when the strangers come? Never, throughout
The whole hideous inverted childhood? Well,
                    We shall find out.

12 January 1973 HW

[197]

Money

Quarterly, is it, money reproaches me:
  'Why do you let me lie here wastefully?
I am all you never had of goods and sex.
  You could get them still by writing a few cheques.'

So I look at others, what they do with theirs:
  They certainly don't keep it upstairs.
By now they've a second house and car and wife:
  Clearly money has something to do with life

– In fact, they've a lot in common, if you enquire:
  You can't put off being young until you retire,
And however you bank your screw, the money you save
  Won't in the end buy you more than a shave.

I listen to money singing. It's like looking down
  From long french windows at a provincial town,
The slums, the canal, the churches ornate and mad
  In the evening sun. It is intensely sad.

19 February 1973 HW

Show Saturday

Grey day for the Show, but cars jam the narrow lanes.
Inside, on the field, judging has started: dogs
(Set their legs back, hold out their tails) and ponies (manes
Repeatedly smoothed, to calm heads); over there, sheep
(Cheviot and Blackface); by the hedge, squealing logs
(Chain Saw Competition). Each has its own keen crowd.
In the main arena, more judges meet by a jeep:
The jumping's on next. Announcements, splutteringly loud,

Clash with the quack of a man with pound notes round his hat
And a lit-up board. There's more than just animals:
Bead-stalls, balloon-men, a Bank; a beer-marquee that
Half-screens a canvas Gents; a tent selling tweed,
And another, jackets. Folks sit about on bales
Like great straw dice. For each scene is linked by spaces
Not given to anything much, where kids scrap, freed,
While their owners stare different ways with incurious faces.

The wrestling starts, late; a wide ring of people; then cars;
Then trees; then pale sky. Two young men in acrobats' tights
And embroidered trunks hug each other; rock over the grass,
Stiff-legged, in a two-man scrum. One falls: they shake hands.
Two more start, one grey-haired: he wins, though. They're not
                                    so much fights
As long immobile strainings that end in unbalance
With one on his back, unharmed, while the other stands
Smoothing his hair. But there are other talents –

The long high tent of growing and making, wired-off
Wood tables past which crowds shuffle, eyeing the scrubbed
                                    spaced
Extrusions of earth: blanch leeks like church candles, six pods of
Broad beans (one split open), dark shining-leafed cabbages –
                                    rows

[199]

Of single supreme versions, followed (on laced
Paper mats) by dairy and kitchen; four brown eggs, four white
                                                                eggs,
Four plain scones, four dropped scones, pure excellences that
                                                              enclose
A recession of skills. And, after them, lambing-sticks, rugs,

Needlework, knitted caps, baskets, all worthy, all well done,
But less than the honeycombs. Outside, the jumping's over.
The young ones thunder their ponies in competition
Twice round the ring; then trick races, Musical Stalls,
Sliding off, riding bareback, the ponies dragged to and fro for
Bewildering requirements, not minding. But now, in the
                                                          background,
Like shifting scenery, horse-boxes move; each crawls
Towards the stock entrance, tilting and swaying, bound

For far-off farms. The pound-note man decamps.
The car park has thinned. They're loading jumps on a truck.
Back now to private addresses, gates and lamps
In high stone one-street villages, empty at dusk,
And side roads of small towns (sports finals stuck
In front doors, allotments reaching down to the railway);
Back now to autumn, leaving the ended husk
Of summer that brought them here for Show Saturday –

The men with hunters, dog-breeding wool-defined women,
Children all saddle-swank, mugfaced middleaged wives
Glaring at jellies, husbands on leave from the garden
Watchful as weasels, car-tuning curt-haired sons –
Back now, all of them, to their local lives:
To names on vans, and business calendars
Hung up in kitchens; back to loud occasions
In the Corn Exchange, to market days in bars,

To winter coming, as the dismantled Show
Itself dies back into the area of work.
Let it stay hidden there like strength, below
Sale-bills and swindling; something people do,
Not noticing how time's rolling smithy-smoke
Shadows much greater gestures; something they share
That breaks ancestrally each year into
Regenerate union. Let it always be there.

3 December 1973 HW

The Life with a Hole in it

When I throw back my head and howl
People (women mostly) say
But you've always done what you want,
You always get your own way
– A perfectly vile and foul
Inversion of all that's been.
What the old ratbags mean
Is I've never done what I don't.

So the shit in the shuttered château
Who does his five hundred words
Then parts out the rest of the day
Between bathing and booze and birds
Is far off as ever, but so
Is that spectacled schoolteaching sod
(Six kids, and the wife in pod,
And her parents coming to stay) . . .

Life is an immobile, locked,
Three-handed struggle between
Your wants, the world's for you, and (worse)
The unbeatable slow machine
That brings what you'll get. Blocked,
They strain round a hollow stasis
Of havings-to, fear, faces.
Days sift down it constantly. Years.

8 August 1974 Poetry Book Society Supplement,
Christmas 1974

Bridge for the Living

The words of a cantata composed by Anthony Hedges to celebrate
the opening of the Humber Bridge, first performed at the City Hall
in Hull on 11 April 1981

Isolate city spread alongside water,
Posted with white towers, she keeps her face
Half-turned to Europe, lonely northern daughter,
Holding through centuries her separate place.

Behind her domes and cranes enormous skies
Of gold and shadows build; a filigree
Of wharves and wires, ricks and refineries,
Her working skyline wanders to the sea.

In her remote three-cornered hinterland
Long white-flowered lanes follow the riverside.
The hills bend slowly seaward, plain gulls stand,
Sharp fox and brilliant pheasant walk, and wide

Wind-muscled wheatfields wash round villages,
Their churches half-submerged in leaf. They lie
Drowned in high summer, cartways and cottages,
The soft huge haze of ash-blue sea close by.

Snow-thickened winter days are yet more still:
Farms fold in fields, their single lamps come on,
Tall church-towers parley, airily audible,
Howden and Beverley, Hedon and Patrington,

While scattered on steep seas, ice-crusted ships
Like errant birds carry her loneliness,
A lighted memory no miles eclipse,
A harbour for the heart against distress.

*

And now this stride into our solitude,
A swallow-fall and rise of one plain line,
A giant step for ever to include
All our dear landscape in a new design.

The winds play on it like a harp; the song,
Sharp from the east, sun-throated from the west,
Will never to one separate shire belong,
But north and south make union manifest.

Lost centuries of local lives that rose
And flowered to fall short where they began
Seem now to reassemble and unclose,
All resurrected in this single span,

Reaching for the world, as our lives do,
As all lives do, reaching that we may give
The best of what we are and hold as true:
Always it is by bridges that we live.

December 1975 Poetry Book Society Supplement,
Christmas 1981

'When first we faced, and touching showed'

When first we faced, and touching showed
How well we knew the early moves,
Behind the moonlight and the frost,
The excitement and the gratitude,
There stood how much our meeting owed
To other meetings, other loves.

The decades of a different life
That opened past your inch-close eyes
Belonged to others, lavished, lost;
Nor could I hold you hard enough
To call my years of hunger-strife
Back for your mouth to colonise.

Admitted: and the pain is real.
But when did love not try to change
The world back to itself – no cost,
No past, no people else at all –
Only what meeting made us feel,
So new, and gentle-sharp, and strange?

20 December 1975

'Morning at last: there in the snow'

Morning at last: there in the snow
Your small blunt footprints come and go.
Night has left no more to show,

Not the candle, half-drunk wine,
Or touching joy; only this sign
Of your life walking into mine.

But when they vanish with the rain
What morning woke to will remain,
Whether as happiness or pain.

1 February 1976

'The little lives of earth and form'

The little lives of earth and form,
Of finding food, and keeping warm,
    Are not like ours, and yet
A kinship lingers nonetheless:
We hanker for the homeliness
    Of den, and hole, and set.

And this identity we feel
– Perhaps not right, perhaps not real –
    Will link us constantly;
I see the rock, the clay, the chalk,
The flattened grass, the swaying stalk,
    And it is you I see.

6 May 1977

Aubade

I work all day, and get half-drunk at night.
Waking at four to soundless dark, I stare.
In time the curtain-edges will grow light.
Till then I see what's really always there:
Unresting death, a whole day nearer now,
Making all thought impossible but how
And where and when I shall myself die.
Arid interrogation: yet the dread
Of dying, and being dead,
Flashes afresh to hold and horrify.

The mind blanks at the glare. Not in remorse
– The good not done, the love not given, time
Torn off unused – nor wretchedly because
An only life can take so long to climb
Clear of its wrong beginnings, and may never;
But at the total emptiness for ever,
The sure extinction that we travel to
And shall be lost in always. Not to be here,
Not to be anywhere,
And soon; nothing more terrible, nothing more true.

This is a special way of being afraid
No trick dispels. Religion used to try,
That vast moth-eaten musical brocade
Created to pretend we never die,
And specious stuff that says *No rational being
Can fear a thing it will not feel*, not seeing
That this is what we fear – no sight, no sound,
No touch or taste or smell, nothing to think with,
Nothing to love or link with,
The anaesthetic from which none come round.

And so it stays just on the edge of vision,
A small unfocused blur, a standing chill
That slows each impulse down to indecision.
Most things may never happen: this one will,
And realisation of it rages out
In furnace-fear when we are caught without
People or drink. Courage is no good:
It means not scaring others. Being brave
Lets no one off the grave.
Death is no different whined at than withstood.

Slowly light strengthens, and the room takes shape.
It stands plain as a wardrobe, what we know,
Have always known, know that we can't escape,
Yet can't accept. One side will have to go.
Meanwhile telephones crouch, getting ready to ring
In locked-up offices, and all the uncaring
Intricate rented world begins to rouse.
The sky is white as clay, with no sun.
Work has to be done.
Postmen like doctors go from house to house.

29 November 1977 Times Literary Supplement,
23 December 1977

'In times when nothing stood'

In times when nothing stood
but worsened, or grew strange,
there was one constant good:
she did not change.

2 March 1978

The Winter Palace

Most people know more as they get older:
I give all that the cold shoulder.

I spent my second quarter-century
Losing what I had learnt at university

And refusing to take in what had happened since.
Now I know none of the names in the public prints,

And am starting to give offence by forgetting faces
And swearing I've never been in certain places.

It will be worth it, if in the end I manage
To blank out whatever it is that is doing the damage.

Then there will be nothing I know.
My mind will fold into itself, like fields, like snow.

1 November 1978

'New eyes each year'

New eyes each year
Find old books here,
And new books, too,
Old eyes renew;
So youth and age
Like ink and page
In this house join,
Minting new coin.

February 1979

'The daily things we do'

The daily things we do
For money or for fun
Can disappear like dew
Or harden and live on.
Strange reciprocity:
The circumstance we cause
In time gives rise to us,
Becomes our memory.

February 1979

The Mower

The mower stalled, twice; kneeling, I found
A hedgehog jammed up against the blades,
Killed. It had been in the long grass.

I had seen it before, and even fed it, once.
Now I had mauled its unobtrusive world
Unmendably. Burial was no help:

Next morning I got up and it did not.
The first day after a death, the new absence
Is always the same; we should be careful

Of each other, we should be kind
While there is still time.

12 June 1979 Humberside (Hull Literary Club magazine)

Autumn 1979

Love Again

Love again: wanking at ten past three
(Surely he's taken her home by now?),
The bedroom hot as a bakery,
The drink gone dead, without showing how
To meet tomorrow, and afterwards,
And the usual pain, like dysentery.

Someone else feeling her breasts and cunt,
Someone else drowned in that lash-wide stare,
And me supposed to be ignorant,
Or find it funny, or not to care,
Even . . . but why put it into words?
Isolate rather this element

That spreads through other lives like a tree
And sways them on in a sort of sense
And say why it never worked for me.
Something to do with violence
A long way back, and wrong rewards,
And arrogant eternity.

20 September 1979

Good for you, Gavin

It's easy to write when you've nothing to write about
    (That is, when you are young),
The heart-shaped hypnotics the press is polite about
    Rise from an unriven tongue.

Later on, attic'd with all-too-familiar
    Tea-chests of truth-sodden grief,
The pages you scrap sound like school songs, or sillier,
    Banal beyond belief.

So good for you, Gavin, for having stayed sprightly
    While keeping your eye on the ball;
Your riotous road-show's like Glenlivet nightly,
    A warming to us all.

26 November 1981 Observer, 29 December 1985

'Dear CHARLES, My Muse, asleep or dead'

Dear CHARLES, My Muse, asleep or dead,
Offers this doggerel instead
To carry from the frozen North
Warm greetings for the twenty-fourth
Of lucky August, best of months
For us, as for that Roman once –
For you're a Leo, same as me
(Isn't it comforting to be
So lordly, selfish, vital, strong?
Or do you think they've got it wrong?),
And may its golden hours portend
As many years for you to spend.

One of the sadder things, I think,
Is how our birthdays slowly sink:
Presents and parties disappear,
The cards grow fewer year by year,
Till, when one reaches sixty-five,
How many care we're still alive?
Ah, CHARLES, be reassured! For you
Make lasting friends with all you do,
And all you write; your truth and sense
We count on as a sure defence
Against the trendy and the mad,
The feeble and the downright bad.
I hope you have a splendid day,
Acclaimed by wheeling gulls at play
And barking seals, sea-lithe and lazy
(My view of Cornwall's rather hazy),
And humans who don't think it sinful
To mark your birthday with a skinful.

Although I'm trying very hard
To sound unlike a birthday card,

That's all this is: so you may find it
Full of all that lies behind it –
Admiration; friendship too;
And hope that in the future you
Reap ever richer revenue.

Poems for Charles Causley, 1982

'Long lion days'

Long lion days
Start with white haze.
By midday you meet
A hammer of heat –
Whatever was sown
Now fully grown,
Whatever conceived
Now fully leaved,
Abounding, ablaze –
O long lion days!

21 July 1982

'By day, a lifted study-storehouse'

By day, a lifted study-storehouse; night
    Converts it to a flattened cube of light.
Whichever's shown, the symbol is the same:
    Knowledge; a University; a name.

October 1983

Party Politics

I never remember holding a full drink.
    My first look shows the level half-way down.
What next? Ration the rest, and try to think
    Of higher things, until mine host comes round?

Some people say, best show an empty glass:
    Someone will fill it. Well, I've tried that too.
You may get drunk, or dry half-hours may pass.
    It seems to turn on where you are. Or who.

Poetry Review, January 1984

EARLY POEMS

1938–45

Winter Nocturne

Mantled in grey, the dusk steals slowly in,
Crossing the dead, dull fields with footsteps cold.
The rain drips drearily; night's fingers spin
A web of drifting mist o'er wood and wold,
As quiet as death. The sky is silent too,
Hard as granite and as fixed as fate.
The pale pond stands; ringed round with rushes few
And draped with leaning trees, it seems to wait
But for the coming of the winter night
Of deep December; blowing o'er the graves
Of faded summers, swift the wind in flight
Ripples its silent face with lapping waves.
The rain falls still: bowing, the woods bemoan;
Dark night creeps in, and leaves the world alone.

The Coventrian, December 1938

Fragment from May

Stands the Spring! – heralded by its bright-clothed
   Trumpeters, of bough and bush and branch;
Pale Winter draws away his white hands, loathed,
   And creeps, a leper, to the cave of time.
Spring the flowers! – a host of nodding gold,
   Leaping and laughing in the boist'rous wind,
Tinged with a yellow as yet not grown old,
   Green and yellow set against the soil.
Flowers the blossom! – loaded, swaying arms
   Of sated stalks, heaped with pink and white
Of fresh youth's cheek; they lightly throw their charms
   Into the fragrance of the deep, wet grass.

The Coventrian, December 1938

Summer Nocturne

Now night perfumes lie upon the air,
As rests the blossom on the loaded bough;
And each deep-drawn breath is redolent
Of all the folded flowers' mingled scent
That rises in confused rapture now.
As from some cool vase filled with petals rare:
And from the silver goblet of the moon
A ghostly light spills down on arched trees,
And filters through their lace to touch the flowers
Among the grass; the silent, dark moon-hours
Flow past, born on the wayward breeze
That wanders through the quiet night of June.
Now time should stop; the web of charm is spun
By the moon's fingers over lawns and flowers;
All pleasures I would give, if this sweet night
Would ever stay, cooled by the pale moonlight;
But no! for in a few white-misted hours
The East must yellow with to-morrow's sun.

The Coventrian, April 1939

'We see the spring breaking across rough stone'

We see the spring breaking across rough stone
  And pause to regard the sky;
But we are pledged to work alone,
  To serve, bow, nor ask if or why.

Summer shimmers over the fishpond.
  We heed it but do not stop
At the may-flies' cloud of mist,
  But penetrate to skeleton beyond.

Autumn is the slow movement;
  We gather our harvest and thank the lofty dusk.
Although glad for the grain, we are
  Aware of the husk.

And winter closes on us like a shroud.
  Whether through windows we shall see spring again
Or not, we are sure to hear the rain
  Chanting its ancient litany, half-aloud.

1939

'Having grown up in shade of Church and State'

Having grown up in shade of Church and State
   Breathing the air of drawing-rooms and scent,
Following the Test Match, tea unsweet in Lent,
   Been given quite a good bat when aged eight,
With black suit, School House tie, and collar white,
   Two hair-brushes and comb, a curl to coax,
He smiles demurely at his uncle's jokes,
   And reads the *Modern Boy* in bed at night.

And when, upon the cricket field, he bats,
   – All perfect strokes – (one sees the dotted line)
And with a careful twelve tries not to vex,
   We hear the voice: 'Y'know, he's good! Why, that's
A graceful player!' True? Perhaps. Benign,
   We diagnose a case of good old sex.

before June 1939

Street Lamps

When night slinks, like a puma, down the sky,
  And the bare, windy streets echo with silence,
Street lamps come out, and lean at corners, awry,
  Casting black shadows, oblique and intense;
So they burn on, impersonal, through the night,
  Hearing the hours slowly topple past
Like cold drops from a glistening stalactite,
  Until grey planes splinter the gloom at last;
Then they go out.

              I think I noticed once
  – T'was morning – one sole street-lamp still bright-lit,
Which, with a senile grin, like an old dunce,
  Vied the blue sky, and tried to rival it;
And, leering pallid though its use was done,
Tried to cast shadows contrary to the sun.

The Coventrian, September 1939

'Why did I dream of you last night?'

Why did I dream of you last night?
Now morning is pushing back hair with grey light
Memories strike home, like slaps in the face:
Raised on elbow, I stare at the pale fog
            beyond the window.

So many things I had thought forgotten
Return to my mind with stranger pain:
– Like letters that arrive addressed to someone
Who left the house so many years ago.

1939

'When the night puts twenty veils'

When the night puts twenty veils
Over the sun, and the west sky pales
    To black its vast sweep:
    Then all is deep
Save where the street lamp gleams upon
                        the rails.

This summertime must be forgot
– It will be, if we would or not –
    Who lost or won?
    Oblivious run:
And sunlight, if it could, would coldly rot.

So. Let me accept the role, and call
Myself the circumstances' tennis-ball:
    We'll bounce: together
    Or not, whether
Either, let no tears silent fall.

before September 1939

'Autumn has caught us in our summer wear'

Autumn has caught us in our summer wear
  Brother, and the day
  Breathes coldly from fields far away
  As white air.
We are cold at our feet, and cold at our throats,
Crouching, cold, deaf to the morning's half-notes.

See, over the fields are coming the girls from the Church,
  Gathering the fruits
  For their Harvest Festival; leaves, berries and roots
  – Such is their search.
I do not think that we shall be
Troubled by their piety.

Tomorrow we shall hear their old bells ringing
  For another year;
  We shall achingcold be here
  – Not singing.
Outside, the frost will bite, thaw, then return;
Inside, the candle will burn.

late 1939

'The hills in their recumbent postures'

The hills in their recumbent postures
  Look into the silent lake;
The bare trees stare across the pastures,
  Waiting for the wind to wake.

As evening dims these sculptured forms
  The mind demands of mortal eye:
'If one should fall among these farms,
  Would not the lake reflect the sky?'

before March 1940

'Nothing significant was really said'

Nothing significant was really said,
Though all agreed the talk superb, and that
The brilliant freshman with his subtle thought
Deserved the praise he won from every side.
All but one declared his future great,
His present sure and happy; they that stayed
Behind, among the ashes, were all stirred
By memory of his words, as sharp as grit.

The one had watched the talk: remembered how
He'd found the genius crying when alone;
Recalled his words: 'O what unlucky streak
Twisting inside me, made me break the line?
What was the rock my gliding childhood struck,
And what bright unreal path has led me here?'

before March 1940

'So you have been, despite parental ban'

So you have been, despite parental ban
　　That would not hear the old demand again;
One who through rain to empty station ran
　　And bought a ticket for the early train.

We heard of all your gain when you had gone,
　　And talked about it when the meal lay done,
The night drawn in, electric light switched on,
　　Your name breathed round the tealeaves and last bun:

How you had laughed, the night before you left;
　　All your potentialities, untried,
Their weakness doffed, became our hero, deft,
　　The don, the climber on the mountain side:

We knew all this absurd, yet were not sad.
　　Today your journey home is nearly done:
That bag above your head, the one you had
　　When seventeen, when you were still a son,

Is labelled now with names we do not know;
　　The gloved hands hang between the static knees,
And show no glee at closing evening's glow –
　　Are you possessor of the sought-for ease?

That name for which you fought – does it quite fit?
　　And is your stubborn silence only tact?
Boys wish to imitate who hear of it –
　　But will you tell them to repeat your act?

March 1940

Spring Warning

And the walker sees the sunlit battlefield
Where winter was fought: the broken sticks in the sun:
    Allotments fresh spaded: here are seen
    The builders on their high scaffold,
        And the red clubhouse flag.
The light, the turf, and all that grows now urge
The uncertain dweller blinking to emerge,
To learn the simpler movements of the jig
And free his gladder impulses from gag.

But there are some who mutter: 'Joy
Is for the simple or the great to feel,
    Neither of which we are.' They file
    The easy chain that bound us, jeer
        At our ancestral forge:
Refuse the sun that flashes from their high
Attic windows, and follow with their eye
The muffled boy, with his compelling badge,
On his serious errand riding to the gorge.

The Coventrian, April 1940

[237]

After-Dinner Remarks

I

A good meal can somewhat repair
   The eatings of slight love;
And now the evening ambles near,
Softly, through the scented air,
Laying by the tautened fear:
   Peace sliding from above.

The trees stand in the setting sun,
   I in their freckled shade
Regard the cavalcade of sin,
Remorse for foolish action done,
That pass like ghosts regardless, in
   A human image made;

And as usual feel rather sad
   At the cathedral spire,
The calling birds that call the dead,
The waving grass that warns the glad,
I think of all that has been said
   About this faint desire;

Of where the other beings move
   Among this evening town,
Innocent of impendent grave,
Happy in their patterned groove,
Who do not need a light to save
   Or cheer when they lie down.

The handsome and the happy, cut
   In one piece from the rock;
With living flesh beneath their coat,
Who cannot their emotions glut,
And know not how to sneer or gloat,
   But only sing or mock,

To these my thoughts swing as a tide
  Turns to its sunny shore;
These I would choose my heart to lead
Instruct and clean, perhaps elide
What evil thought was bearing seed,
  And must spring up no more.

II

Pondering reflections as
  Complex and deep as these,
I saw my life as in a glass:
Set to music (negro jazz),
Coloured by culture and by gas,
  The idea of a kiss:

Contemptible: I quite agree,
  Now that the evening dies,
The sky proceeds from blue to grey
By imperceptible degree
And light and curtains drawn allay
  The vastness of the skies.

Stigmatised the exile who
  Cannot go from his land,
I in a dream of sea and hay,
Of kissing wind and merging blue
Think what I could have won today
  By stretching out my hand,

The challenge that I could proclaim
  The vows that I could swear;
Equipment to attempt the climb,
Or by straight love the world to tame,
What gesture in the face of time
  Could I have fashioned there.

[239]

Though living is a dreadful thing
And a dreadful thing is it –
Life the niggard will not thank,
She will not teach who will not sing,
And what serves, on the final bank,
Our logic and our wit?

III

Who for events to come to him
May wait until his death:
Life will not violate his home
But leaves him to his evenings dim;
When all the world starts out to roam,
She lets him save his breath.

What does he gain? Alas, relief
Shrivels with his youth;
He will forget the way to laugh,
Cut off by his mental reef
From music hall and tall giraffe –
He will distort the truth.

Against these facts this can be set –
We do not make ourselves:
There is no point in such deceit,
To introspectively regret
Can never our defect defeat,
Or mend our broken halves.

Those who are born to rot, decay –
And am I one of these?
A keyhole made without a key,
A poem none can read or say,
A gate none open wide to see
The fountains and the trees.

Excuse for doing nothing, yes –
 But I can still point out
That one can will and will for years
Be neither Aaron nor a Tess
But only see, through staling tears,
 A quickly-spawning doubt.

IV

Choose what you can: I do remain
 As neuter: and meanwhile
Exploding shrapnel bursts the men
Who thought perhaps they would disdain
The world that from its reechy den
 Emerges with a smile;

All the familiar horrors we
 Associate with others
Are coming fast along our way:
The wind is warning in our tree
And morning papers still betray
 The shrieking of the mothers.

And so, while summer on this day
 Enacts her dress rehearsals,
Let us forget who has to die,
Swim in the delicious bay,
Experience emotion by
 The marvellous cathedrals;

Sad at our incompetence
 Yet powerless to resist
The eating bane of thought that weans
Us to a serious birthday whence
We realise the sterile 'teens
 And what we shall have missed

[241]

When all the lovely people that
    Instinct should have obeyed
Have passed us in our tub of thought,
As on this evening when we sat
Devoid of help from simple 'ought'
    Or resolution's aid.

Around, the night drops swiftly down
    Its veils; does not condemn
Or praise the different actions done.
The hour that strikes across the town
Caresses all and injures none
    As sleep approaches them.

before June 1940

Ultimatum

But we must build our walls, for what we are
Necessitates it, and we must construct
The ship to navigate behind them, there.
Hopeless to ignore, helpless instruct
For any term of time beyond the years
That warn us of the need for emigration:
Exploded the ancient saying: Life is yours.

For on our island is no railway station,
There are no tickets for the Vale of Peace,
No docks where trading ships and seagulls pass.

Remember stories you read when a boy
– The shipwrecked sailor gaining safety by
His knife, treetrunk, and lianas – for now
You must escape, or perish saying no.

June ? 1940 Listener, 28 November 1940

Midsummer Night, 1940

The sun falls behind Wales; the towns and hills
Sculptured on England, wait again for night
As a deserted beach the tide that smoothes

Its rumpled surface flat: as pale as moths
Faces from factory pass home, for what respite
Home offers: crowds vacate the public halls:

And everywhere the stifling mass of night
Swamps the bright nervous day, and puts it out.
In other times, when heavy ploughmen snored,

And only some among the wealthy sneered,
On such a night as this twilight and doubt
Would mingle, and the night would not

Be day's exhaustion; there would drift about
Strange legends of the bridge across the weir,
Rings found in the grass, with undertone

Of darker terror, stories of the tarn,
The horned stranger, a pervading fear
No jolly laugh disperses. But

We, on this midsummer night, can sneer
In union at mind that could confuse
The moon and cheese, or trust in lightfoot images,

And point with conscious pride to our monstrosities
– Gained by no cerebral subterfuge,
Yet more convincing – a compulsory snare,

Expending of resources for the use
Of all the batty guardians of pain
– With no acknowledgment of pleasure, even –

The angels yawning in an empty heaven;
Alternate shows of dynamite and rain;
And choosing forced on free will: fire or ice.

June 1940

'As a war in years of peace'

As a war in years of peace
Or in war an armistice
Or a father's death, just so
Our parting was not visualized
When from the further side I gazed
Occasionally, as likely sorrow,

For parting is no single act
Scenery-shifting for the next,
Parting is a trailing streamer,
Lingering like leaves in autumn
Thinning at the winter's comb –
No more impressive nor supremer;

If so, then still is less than death,
The only parting; on a hearth
Or passing street, always the meeting
And the wondering brain and eye
Quickly consulting memory
To follow or precede the greeting.

Only another case, perhaps,
Arranges our predestined shapes:
That of brilliant passing liner,
Or the miraculous interpretation
Of the simple composition –
Jewels life throws up like a miner.

And so, being caught quite unawares
By petition for some gracious tears,
I ponder on the consequence
Of never seeing this, nor saying
What, remembered, still seems glowing
As all of you. Indifference?

1940

Schoolmaster

He sighed with relief. He had got the job. He was safe.
Putting on his gown, he prepared for the long years to come
That he saw, stretching like aisles of stone
Before him. He prepared for the unreal life
Of exercises, marks, honour, speech days and games,
And the interesting and pretty animals that inspired it all,
And made him a god. No, he would never fail.

Others, of course, had often spoken of the claims
Of living: they were merely desperate.
His defence of Youth and Service silenced it.

It was acted as he planned: grown old and favourite,
With most Old Boys he was quite intimate –
For though he never realised it, he
Dissolved. (Like sugar in a cup of tea.)

1940

'There is no language of destruction'

There is no language of destruction for
The use of the chaotic; silence the only
Path for those hysterical and lonely.
That upright beauty cannot banish fear,
Or wishing help the weak to gain the fair
Is reason for it: that the skilled event,
Gaining applause, cannot a death prevent,
Short-circuits impotent who travel far.

And no word can be spoken of which the sense
Does not accuse and contradict at once.
And he gets no assistance from the world
Which will not help his looking into words,
Nor will the lovely, gay as any leaf,
Assuage his anguish. And the lions laugh.

1940

Last Will and Testament

Anxious to publicise and pay our dues
Contracted here, we, Bernard Noel Hughes
And Philip Arthur Larkin, do desire

To requite and to reward those whom we choose;
To thank our friends, before our time expire,
And those whom, if not friends, we yet admire.

First, our corporeal remains we give
Unto the Science Sixth – demonstrative
Of physical fitness – for minute dissection;

Trusting that they will generously forgive
Any trifling lapses from perfection,
And give our viscera their close attention.

– With one exception: we bequeath our ears
To the Musical Society, and hope
It finds out why they loathed the panatrope –

(And, however pointed it appears,
We leave the wash-bowls twenty cakes of soap)
Item, herewith to future pioneers

In realms of knowledge, we bequeath our books,
And woe pursue who to a master quotes
The funnier of our witty marginal notes.

Likewise, we leave the Modern Sixth the jokes
This year has fostered, and to him who croaks
Of Higher School Certificates, ten sore throats.

Item, our school reports we leave the Staff,
To give them, as we hope, a hearty laugh;
And Kipling's 'If' to hang upon their wall.

Sympathy for the impossible task
Of teaching us to swim the six-beat crawl
We leave our swimming master. Item, all

Our *Magnets* and our *Wizards* we consign
To the Librarian in the cause of Culture
And may his Library flourish well in future;

Next (now the troops have taken their departure)
With ever-grateful hearts we do assign
To our French master, all the Maginot Line.

Essays, and our notes on style and diction,
We leave our English master, confident
He won't consider them as an infliction.

Our German master, for the sore affliction
Of teaching us, we humbly present
With an Iron Cross (First Class, but slightly bent);

To the Art Master, as the only one
Appreciative (and, Philistines to thwart)
We leave a blue cap and four ties that stun:

And all the Scholarships we never won
We give to those who want things of that sort:
And to the Savings Groups . . . our full support.

Our Games Master we leave some high-jump stands
– The reason why we know he understands –
And to the Carpenter the grass he's mown.

To Paul Montgomery, a sturdy comb
To discipline his rough and ruddy strands;
And Mr H. B. Gould we leave . . . alone.

We leave our Latin cribs to William Rider,
And may his shadow never disappear;
To the Zoologists, a common spider;

And, for their services throughout the year,
To the Air Defence Cadets a model glider;
And to the First XV a cask of beer.

Item, to Percy Slater we now send
A candle he can burn at either end,
And hours of toil without the ill-effects;

Our badges we resign to future Prefects,
The lines-book, too; to F. G. Smith, our friend,
We leave a compact and a bottle of Cutex;

And all the paper that we never needed
For this *Coventrian*, to Ian Fraser,
And may he triumph where we've not succeeded:

To his subordinates, an ink eraser . . .
And this Magazine itself? Well, there's always a
Lot of people queer enough to read it.

Herewith we close, with Time's apology
For the ephemeral injury,
On this 26th of July, 1940.

The Coventrian, September 1940

[252]

'Out in the lane I pause'

Out in the lane I pause: the night
Impenetrable round me stands,
And overhead, where roofline ends,
　　　The starless sky
Black as a bridge: the only light
Gleams from the little railway
　　　That runs nearby.

From the steep road that travels down
Towards the shops, I hear the feet
Of lonely walkers in the night
　　　Or lingering pairs;
Girls and their soldiers from the town
Who in the shape of future years
　　　Have equal shares;

But not tonight are questions posed
By them; no, nor the bleak escape
Through doubt from endless love and hope
　　　To hate and terror;
Each in their double Eden closed
They fail to see the gardener there
　　　Has planted Error;

Nor can their wish for quiet days
Be granted; though their motions kiss
This evening, and make happiness
　　　Plain as a book,
They must pursue their separate ways
And flushed with puzzled tears, turn back
　　　Their puzzled look.

And if, as of gipsy at a fair,
Sorry, I inquire for them

If things are really what they seem,
      The open sky
And all the gasping, withered air
Can only answer: 'It is so'
      In brief reply.

So through the dark I walk, and feel
The ending year about me lapse,
Dying, into its formal shapes
      Of field and tree;
And think I hear its faint appeal
Addressed to all who seek for joy,
      But mainly me:

'From those constellations turn
Your eyes, and sleep; for every man
Is living; and for peace upon
      His life should rest;
This must everybody learn
For mutual happiness; that trust
      Alone is best.'

December 1940

New Year Poem

The short afternoon ends, and the year is over;
Above trees at the end of the garden the sky is unchanged,
An endless sky; and the wet streets, as ever,
Between standing houses are empty and unchallenged.
From roads where men go home I walk apart
– The buses bearing their loads away from works,
Through the dusk the bicycles coming home from bricks –
There evening like a derelict lorry is alone and mute.

These houses are deserted, felt over smashed windows,
No milk on the step, a note pinned to the door
Telling of departure: only shadows
Move when in the day the sun is seen for an hour,
Yet to me this decaying landscape has its uses:
To make me remember, who am always inclined to forget,
That there is always a changing at the root,
And a real world in which time really passes.

For even together, outside this shattered city
And its obvious message, if we had lived in that peace
Where the enormous years pass over lightly
– Yes, even there, if I looked into your face
Expecting a word or a laugh on the old conditions,
It would not be a friend who met my eye,
Only a stranger would smile and turn away,
Not one of the two who first performed these actions.

For sometimes it is shown to me in dreams
The Eden that all wish to recreate
Out of their living, from their favourite times;
The miraculous play where all their dead take part,
Once more articulate; or the distant ones
They will never forget because of an autumn talk

By a railway, an occasional glimpse in a public park,
Any memory for the most part depending on chance.

And seeing this through that I know that to be wrong,
Knowing by the flower the root that seemed so harmless
Dangerous; and all must take their warning
From these brief dreams of unsuccessful charms,
Their aloof visions of delight, where Desire
And Fear work hand-in-glove like medicals
To produce the same results. The bells
That we used to await will not be rung this year,

So it is better to sleep and leave the bottle unopened;
Tomorrow in the offices the year on the stamps will be altered;
Tomorrow new diaries consulted, new calendars stand;
With such small adjustments life will again move forward
Implicating us all; and the voice of the living be heard:
'It is to us that you should turn your straying attention;
Us who need you, and are affected by your fortune;
Us you should love and to whom you should give your word.'

31 December 1940

Story

Tired of a landscape known too well when young:
The deliberate shallow hills, the boring birds
Flying past rocks; tired of remembering
The village children and their naughty words,
He abandoned his small holding and went South,
Recognised at once his wished-for lie
In the inhabitants' attractive mouth,
The church beside the marsh, the hot blue sky.

Settled. And in this mirage lived his dreams,
The friendly bully, saint, or lovely chum
According to his moods. Yet he at times
Would think about his village, and would wonder
If the children and the rocks were still the same.

But he forgot all this as he grew older.

Cherwell, 13 February 1941

'The house on the edge of the serious wood'

The house on the edge of the serious wood
        Was aware, was aware
        Of why he came there,
And the reticent toad never told what it knew
When from the wet bracken it saw him pass through;
And round the next corner a tree poked its head:
'He's coming; be careful; pretend to be dead.'

Down on the river the swans sailed on,
        And on flowed the river
        For ever and ever
Over the interlocked counties and shires,
But never revealed that they knew his desires;
Reflected him walking alone in the sun,
And smiled at each other when he had gone.

On the school field at the edge of the town
        Where surely the secret
        Would not be so sacred
And might any moment materialise
He looked at the juniors with hopeful eyes
– But none of them moved until he had gone,
Then the game went on, the game went on.

No, neither the wood nor river nor child
        Showed as they should
        The True and the Good
Like a valley in blossom or plain as snow,
For they rather resented what he wished them to do;
Imagined he wished them to mirror his mind
That grew like a sapling and orchid combined;

But for once they were wrong: for the motives of acts
        Are rarely the same

As their name, as their name;
And they were not aware of his previous tours
Upon southern Alps, across northern moors,
Seeking in one place always another,
And travelling further from mother, from mother:

No, they were not told of the willing lanes,
        The black mill-pond
        Of which he was fond;
The warm and the narrow, the shadowed, the queer
As opposed to the open, the broad and the clear,
These strange dark patterns of his heart's designs
That would only respond to secret signs

That signalled in attics and gardens like Hope,
        And ever would pass
        From address to address,
As he watched from windows in the failing light
For his world that was always just out of sight
Where weakness was part of the ordinary landscape
And the friendly road knew his footstep, his footstep.

before April 1941

'Time and Space were only their disguises'

Time and Space were only their disguises
Under which their hatred chose its shapes
From swords in bushes, flowers like periscopes,
And mirrors that revealed themselves as faces.

And later, clouds flew past me as I sat;
Stations like ships swam up to meet the train
And bowed; all time was equal like the sun;
Each landscape was elaborately set.

But now this blackened city in the snow
Argues a will that cannot be my own,
And one not wished for: points to show

Time in his little cinema of the heart
Giving a première to Hate and Pain;
And Space urbanely keeping us apart.

before April 1941

May Weather

A month ago in fields
Rehearsals were begun;
The stage that summer builds
And confidently holds
Was floodlit by the sun
And habited by men.

But parts were not correct:
The gestures of the crowd
Invented to attract
Need practice to perfect,
And balancing of cloud
With sunlight must be made;

So awkward was this May
Then training to prepare
Summer's impressive lie –
Upon whose every day
So many ruined are
May could not make aware.

Cherwell, 5 June 1941

Conscript

for James Ballard Sutton

The ego's county he inherited
From those who tended it like farmers; had
All knowledge that the study merited,
The requisite contempt of good and bad;

But one Spring day his land was violated;
A bunch of horsemen curtly asked his name,
Their leader in a different dialect stated
A war was on for which he was to blame,

And he must help them. The assent he gave
Was founded on desire for self-effacement
In order not to lose his birthright; brave,
For nothing would be easier than replacement,

Which would not give him time to follow further
The details of his own defeat and murder.

Phoenix, October–November 1941, TNS

A Writer

'Interesting, but futile,' said his diary,
Where day by day his movements were recorded
And nothing but his loves received inquiry;
He knew, of course, no actions were rewarded,
There were no prizes: though the eye could see
Wide beauty in a motion or a pause,
It need expect no lasting salary
Beyond the bowels' momentary applause.

He lived for years and never was surprised:
A member of his foolish, lying race
Explained away their vices: realised
It was a gift that he possessed alone:
To look the world directly in the face;
The face he did not see to be his own.

Cherwell, 8 May 1941

Observation

Only in books the flat and final happens,
Only in dreams we meet and interlock,
The hand impervious to nervous shock,
The future proofed against our vain suspense;

But since the tideline of the incoming past
Is where we walk, and it is air we breathe,
Remember then our only shape is death
When mask and face are nailed apart at last.

Range-finding laughter, and ambush of tears,
Machine-gun practice on the heart's desires
Speak of a government of medalled fears.

Shake, wind, the branches of their crooked wood,
Where much is picturesque but nothing good,
And nothing can be found for poor men's fires.

Oxford University Labour Club Bulletin, 22 November 1941

'This was your place of birth, this daytime palace'

This was your place of birth, this daytime palace,
This miracle of glass, whose every hall
The light as music fills, and on your face
Shines petal-soft; sunbeams are prodigal
To show you pausing at a picture's edge
To puzzle out the name, or with a hand
Resting a second on a random page –

The clouds cast moving shadows on the land.

Are you prepared for what the night will bring?
The stranger who will never show his face,
But asks admittance; will you greet your doom
As final; set him loaves and wine; knowing
The game is finished when he plays his ace,
And overturn the table and go into the next room?

Cherwell, 28 February 1942, TNS

[265]

Disintegration

Time running beneath the pillow wakes
Lovers entrained who in the name of love
Were promised the steeples and fanlights of a dream;
Joins the renters of each single room
Across the tables to observe a life
Dissolving in the acid of their sex;

Time that scatters hair upon a head
Spreads the ice sheet on the shaven lawn;
Signing an annual permit for the frost
Ploughs the stubble in the land at last
To introduce the unknown to the known
And only by politeness make them breed;

Time over the roofs of what has nearly been
Circling, a migratory, static bird,
Predicts no change in future's lancing shape,
And daylight shows the streets still tangled up;
Time points the simian camera in the head
Upon confusion to be seen and seen.

Oxford University Labour Club Bulletin, February 1942

'I dreamed of an out-thrust arm of land'

I dreamed of an out-thrust arm of land
Where gulls blew over a wave
That fell along miles of sand;
And the wind climbed up the caves
To tear at a dark-faced garden
Whose black flowers were dead,
And broke round a house we slept in,
A drawn blind and a bed.

I was sleeping, and you woke me
To walk on the chilled shore
Of a night with no memory,
Till your voice forsook my ear
Till your two hands withdrew
And I was empty of tears,
On the edge of a bricked and streeted sea
And a cold hill of stars.

Arabesque, Hilary term 1943, TNS

Mythological Introduction

A white girl lay on the grass
With her arms held out for love;
Her goldbrown hair fell down her face,
And her two lips move:

> See, I am the whitest cloud that strays
> Through a deep sky:
> I am your senses' crossroads,
> Where the four seasons lie.

She rose up in the middle of the lawn
And spread her arms wide;
And the webbed earth where she had lain
Had eaten away her side.

Arabesque, Hilary term 1943

A Stone Church Damaged by a Bomb

Planted deeper than roots,
This chiselled, flung-up faith
Runs and leaps against the sky,
A prayer killed into stone
Among the always-dying trees;
Windows throw back the sun
And hands are folded in their work at peace,
Though where they lie
The dead are shapeless in the shapeless earth.

Because, though taller the elms,
It forever rejects the soil,
Because its suspended bells
Beat when the birds are dumb,
And men are buried, and leaves burnt
Every indifferent autumn,
I have looked on that proud front
And the calm locked into walls,
I have worshipped that whispering shell.

Yet the wound, O see the wound
This petrified heart has taken,
Because, created deathless,
Nothing but death remained
To scatter magnificence;
And now what scaffolded mind
Can rebuild experience
As coral is set budding under seas,
Though none, O none sees what patterns it is making?

Oxford Poetry 1942–3, June 1943

Femmes Damnées

The fire is ash: the early morning sun
Outlines the patterns on the curtains, drawn
The night before. The milk's been on the step,
The *Guardian* in the letter-box, since dawn.

Upstairs, the beds have not been touched, and thence
Builders' estates and the main road are seen,
With labourers, petrol-pumps, a Green Line bus,
And plots of cabbages set in between.

But the living-room is ruby: there upon
Cushions from Harrods, strewn in tumbled heaps
Around the floor, smelling of smoke and wine,
Rosemary sits. Her hands are clasped. She weeps.

She stares about her: round the decent walls
(The ribbon lost, her pale gold hair falls down)
Sees books and photos: 'Dance'; 'The Rhythmic Life';
Miss Rachel Wilson in a cap and gown.

Stretched out before her, Rachel curls and curves,
Eyelids and lips apart, her glances filled
With satisfied ferocity; she smiles,
As beasts smile on the prey they have just killed.

The marble clock has stopped. The curtained sun
Burns on: the room grows hot. There, it appears,
A vase of flowers has spilt, and soaked away.
The only sound heard is the sound of tears.

1943 Sycamore Broadsheet 27, 1978

[270]

The School in August

The cloakroom pegs are empty now,
And locked the classroom door,
The hollow desks are dimmed with dust,
And slow across the floor
A sunbeam creeps between the chairs
Till the sun shines no more.

Who did their hair before this glass?
Who scratched 'Elaine loves Jill'
One drowsy summer sewing-class
With scissors on the sill?
Who practised this piano
Whose notes are now so still?

Ah, notices are taken down,
And scorebooks stowed away,
And seniors grow tomorrow
From the juniors today,
And even swimming groups can fade,
Games mistresses turn grey.

1943?

'All catches alight'
to Bruce Montgomery

All catches alight
At the spread of spring:
Birds crazed with flight
Branches that fling
Leaves up to the light –
Every one thing,
Shape, colour and voice,
Cries out, Rejoice!
    A drum taps: a wintry drum.

Gull, grass and girl
In air, earth and bed
Join the long whirl
Of all the resurrected,
Gather up and hurl
Far out beyond the dead
What life they can control –
All runs back to the whole.
    A drum taps: a wintry drum.

What beasts now hesitate
Clothed in cloudless air,
In whom desire stands straight?
What ploughman halts his pair
To kick a broken plate
Or coin turned up by the share?
What lovers worry much
That a ghost bids them touch?
    A drum taps: a wintry drum.

Let the wheel spin out,
Till all created things
With shout and answering shout

Cast off rememberings;
Let it all come about
Till centuries of springs
And all their buried men
Stand on the earth again.
    A drum taps: a wintry drum.

early 1944 POW, TNS

'The moon is full tonight'

The moon is full tonight
And hurts the eyes,
It is so definite and bright.
What if it has drawn up
All quietness and certitude of worth
Wherewith to fill its cup,
Or mint a second moon, a paradise? –
For they are gone from earth.

1943–4 POW, TNS

[274]

'The horns of the morning'

The horns of the morning
Are blowing, are shining,
The meadows are bright
    With the coldest dew;
The dawn reassembles,
Like the clash of gold cymbals
The sky spreads its vans out
    The sun hangs in view.

Here, where no love is,
All that was hopeless
And kept me from sleeping
    Is frail and unsure;
For never so brilliant,
Neither so silent
Nor so unearthly, has
    Earth grown before.

1943–4 POW, TNS

[275]

'I put my mouth'

I put my mouth
Close to running water:
Flow north, flow south,
It will not matter,
It is not love you will find.

I told the wind:
It took away my words:
It is not love you will find,
Only the bright-tongued birds,
Only a moon with no home.

It is not love you will find:
You have no limbs
Crying for stillness, you have no mind
Trembling with seraphim,
You have no death to come.

1943–4 POW, TNS, ITGOL

'The bottle is drunk out by one'

The bottle is drunk out by one;
At two, the book is shut;
At three, the lovers lie apart,
Love and its commerce done;
And now the luminous watch-hands
Show after four o'clock,
Time of night when straying winds
Trouble the dark.

And I am sick for want of sleep;
So sick, that I can half-believe
The soundless river pouring from the cave
Is neither strong, nor deep;
Only an image fancied in conceit.
I lie and wait for morning, and the birds,
The first steps going down the unswept street,
Voices of girls with scarves around their heads.

1943–4 POW, TNS

'I see a girl dragged by the wrists'

I see a girl dragged by the wrists
Across a dazzling field of snow,
And there is nothing in me that resists.
Once it would not be so;
Once I should choke with powerless jealousies;
But now I seem devoid of subtlety,
As simple as the things I see,
Being no more, no less, than two weak eyes.

There is snow everywhere,
Snow in one blinding light.
Even snow smudged in her hair
As she laughs and struggles, and pretends to fight;
And still I have no regret;
Nothing so wild, nothing so glad as she
Rears up in me,
And would not, though I watched an hour yet.

So I walk on. Perhaps what I desired
– That long and sickly hope, someday to be
As she is – gave a flicker and expired;
For the first time I'm content to see
What poor mortar and bricks
I have to build with, knowing that I can
Never in seventy years be more a man
Than now – a sack of meal upon two sticks.

So I walk on. And yet the first brick's laid.
Else how should two old ragged men
Clearing the drifts with shovels and a spade
Bring up my mind to fever-pitch again?
How should they sweep the girl clean from my heart,
With no more done

[278]

Than to stand coughing in the sun,
Then stoop and shovel snow onto a cart?

The beauty dries my throat.
Now they express
All that's content to wear a worn-out coat,
All actions done in patient hopelessness,
All that ignores the silences of death,
Thinking no further than the hand can hold,
All that grows old,
Yet works on uselessly with shortened breath.

Damn all explanatory rhymes!
To be that girl! – but that's impossible;
For me the task's to learn the many times
When I must stoop, and throw a shovelful:
I must repeat until I live the fact
That everything's remade
With shovel and spade;
That each dull day and each despairing act

Builds up the crags from which the spirit leaps
– The beast most innocent
That is so fabulous it never sleeps;
If I can keep against all argument
Such image of a snow-white unicorn,
Then as I pray it may for sanctuary
Descend at last to me,
And put into my hand its golden horn.

early 1944 POW, TNS

'Love, we must part now'

Love, we must part now: do not let it be
Calamitous and bitter. In the past
There has been too much moonlight and self-pity:
Let us have done with it: for now at last
Never has sun more boldly paced the sky,
Never were hearts more eager to be free,
To kick down worlds, lash forests; you and I
No longer hold them; we are husks, that see
The grain going forward to a different use.

There is regret. Always, there is regret.
But it is better that our lives unloose,
As two tall ships, wind-mastered, wet with light,
Break from an estuary with their courses set,
And waving part, and waving drop from sight.

1943–4 POW, TNS

'Morning has spread again'

Morning has spread again
Through every street,
And we are strange again;
For should we meet
How can I tell you that
Last night you came
Unbidden, in a dream?
And how forget
That we had worn down love good-humouredly,
Talking in fits and starts
As friends, as they will be
Who have let passion die within their hearts.
Now, watching the red east expand,
I wonder love can have already set
In dreams, when we've not met
More times than I can number on one hand.

1943–4 POW, TNS

'Heaviest of flowers, the head'

Heaviest of flowers, the head
Forever hangs above a stormless bed;
Hands that the heart can govern
Shall be at last by darker hands unwoven;
Every exultant sense
Unstrung to silence –
The sun drift away.

And all the memories that best
Run back beyond this season of unrest
Shall lie upon the earth
That gave them birth.
Like fallen apples, they will lose
Their sweetness at the bruise,
And then decay.

1943–4 POW, TNS, ITGOL

[282]

'So through that unripe day you bore your head'

So through that unripe day you bore your head,
And the day was plucked and tasted bitter,
As if still cold among the leaves. Instead,
It was your severed image that grew sweeter,
That floated, wing-stiff, focused in the sun
Along uncertainty and gales of shame
Blown out before I slept. Now you are one
I dare not think alive: only a name
That chimes occasionally, as a belief
Long since embedded in the static past.

Summer broke and drained. Now we are safe.
The days lose confidence, and can be faced
Indoors. This is your last, meticulous hour,
Cut, gummed; pastime of a provincial winter.

1943–4 POW, TNS

[283]

Dawn

To wake, and hear a cock
Out of the distance crying,
To pull the curtains back
And see the clouds flying –
How strange it is
For the heart to be loveless, and as cold as these.

1943–4 TNS

'Kick up the fire, and let the flames break loose'

Kick up the fire, and let the flames break loose
To drive the shadows back;
Prolong the talk on this or that excuse,
Till the night comes to rest
While some high bell is beating two o'clock.
Yet when the guest
Has stepped into the windy street, and gone,
Who can confront
The instantaneous grief of being alone?
Or watch the sad increase
Across the mind of this prolific plant,
Dumb idleness?

1943–4 TNS

Winter

In the field, two horses,
Two swans on the river,
While a wind blows over
A waste of thistles
Crowded like men;
And now again
My thoughts are children
With uneasy faces
That awake and rise
Beneath running skies
From buried places.

For the line of a swan
Diagonal on water
Is the cold of winter,
And each horse like a passion
Long since defeated
Lowers its head,
And oh, they invade
My cloaked-up mind
Till memory unlooses
Its brooch of faces –
Streams far behind.

Then the whole heath whistles
In the leaping wind,
And shrivelled men stand
Crowding like thistles
To one fruitless place;
Yet still the miracles
Exhume in each face
Strong silken seed,

That to the static
Gold winter sun throws back
Endless and cloudless pride.

1943–4 TNS, ITGOL

'Like the train's beat'

Like the train's beat
Swift language flutters the lips
Of the Polish airgirl in the corner seat.
The swinging and narrowing sun
Lights her eyelashes, shapes
Her sharp vivacity of bone.
Hair, wild and controlled, runs back:
And gestures like these English oaks
Flash past the windows of her foreign talk.

The train runs on through wilderness
Of cities. Still the hammered miles
Diversify behind her face.
And all humanity of interest
Before her angled beauty falls,
As whorling notes are pressed
In a bird's throat, issuing meaningless
Through written skies; a voice
Watering a stony place.

1943–4 TNS

Nursery Tale

All I remember is
The horseman, the moonlit hedges,
The hoofbeats shut suddenly in the yard,
The hand finding the door unbarred:
And I recall the room where he was brought,
Hung black and candlelit; a sort
Of meal laid out in mockery; for though
His place was set, there was no more
Than one unpolished pewter dish, that bore
The battered carcase of a carrion crow.

So every journey that I make
Leads me, as in the story he was led,
To some new ambush, to some fresh mistake:
So every journey I begin foretells
A weariness of daybreak, spread
With carrion kisses, carrion farewells.

1943–4 TNS

The Dancer

Butterfly
Or falling leaf,
Which ought I to imitate
In my dancing?

And if she were to admit
The world weaved by her feet
Is leafless, is incomplete?
And if she abandoned it,
Broke the pivoted dance,
Set loose the audience?
Then would the moon go raving,
The moon, the anchorless
Moon go swerving
Down at the earth for a catastrophic kiss.

1943–4 TNS

'To write one song, I said'

To write one song, I said,
As sad as the sad wind
That walks around my bed,
Having one simple fall
As a candle-flame swells, and is thinned,
As a curtain stirs by the wall
– For this I must visit the dead.
Headstone and wet cross,
Paths where the mourners tread,
A solitary bird,
These call up the shade of loss,
Shape word to word.

That stones would shine like gold
Above each sodden grave,
This, I had not foretold,
Nor the birds' clamour, nor
The image morning gave
Of more and ever more,
As some vast seven-piled wave,
Mane-flinging, manifold,
Streams at an endless shore.

1943–4 TNS

Ugly Sister

I will climb thirty steps to my room,
Lie on my bed;
Let the music, the violin, cornet and drum
Drowse from my head.

Since I was not bewitched in adolescence
And brought to love,
I will attend to the trees and their gracious silence,
To winds that move.

1943–4 TNS

'One man walking a deserted platform'

One man walking a deserted platform;
Dawn coming, and rain
Driving across a darkening autumn;
One man restlessly waiting a train
While round the streets the wind runs wild,
Beating each shuttered house, that seems
Folded full of the dark silk of dreams,
A shell of sleep cradling a wife or child.

Who can this ambition trace,
To be each dawn perpetually journeying?
To trick this hour when lovers re-embrace
With the unguessed-at heart riding
The winds as gulls do? What lips said
Starset and cockcrow call the dispossessed
On to the next desert, lest
Love sink a grave round the still-sleeping head?

1944 TNS, ITGOL (as 'Getaway')

[293]

'If hands could free you, heart'

If hands could free you, heart,
　　Where would you fly?
Far, beyond every part
Of earth this running sky
Makes desolate? Would you cross
City and hill and sea,
　　If hands could set you free?

I would not lift the latch;
　　For I could run
Through fields, pit-valleys, catch
All beauty under the sun –
Still end in loss:
I should find no bent arm, no bed
　　To rest my head.

1943–4 TNS

'This is the first thing'

This is the first thing
I have understood:
Time is the echo of an axe
Within a wood.

1943–4 TNS

'Is it for now or for always'

Is it for now or for always,
The world hangs on a stalk?
Is it a trick or a trysting-place,
The woods we have found to walk?

Is it a mirage or miracle,
Your lips that lift at mine:
And the suns like a juggler's juggling-balls,
Are they a sham or a sign?

Shine out, my sudden angel,
Break fear with breast and brow,
I take you now and for always,
For always is always now.

1943–4 TNS

'Pour away that youth'

Pour away that youth
That overflows the heart
Into hair and mouth;
Take the grave's part,
Tell the bone's truth.

Throw away that youth
That jewel in the head
That bronze in the breath;
Walk with the dead
For fear of death.

1943–4 TNS

'If grief could burn out'

If grief could burn out
Like a sunken coal,
The heart would rest quiet,
The unrent soul
Be still as a veil;
But I have watched all night

The fire grow silent,
The grey ash soft:
And I stir the stubborn flint
The flames have left,
And grief stirs, and the deft
Heart lies impotent.

5 October 1944 TNS

'Within the dream you said'

Within the dream you said:
Let us kiss then,
In this room, in this bed,
But when all's done
We must not meet again.

Hearing this last word,
There was no lambing-night,
No gale-driven bird
Nor frost-encircled root
As cold as my heart.

12 October 1944 TNS, ITGOL

Night-Music

At one the wind rose,
And with it the noise
Of the black poplars.

Long since had the living
By a thin twine
Been led into their dreams
Where lanterns shine
Under a still veil
Of falling streams;
Long since had the dead
Become untroubled
In the light soil.
There were no mouths
To drink of the wind,
Nor any eyes
To sharpen on the stars'
Wide heaven-holding,
Only the sound
Long sibilant-muscled trees
Were lifting up, the black poplars.

And in their blazing solitude
The stars sang in their sockets through the night:
'Blow bright, blow bright
The coal of this unquickened world.'

12 October 1944 TNS, ITGOL

'Climbing the hill within the deafening wind'

Climbing the hill within the deafening wind
The blood unfurled itself, was proudly borne
High over meadows where white horses stood;
Up the steep woods it echoed like a horn
Till at the summit under shining trees
It cried: Submission is the only good;
Let me become an instrument sharply stringed
For all things to strike music as they please.

How to recall such music, when the street
Darkens? Among the rain and stone places
I find only an ancient sadness falling,
Only hurrying and troubled faces,
The walking of girls' vulnerable feet,
The heart in its own endless silence kneeling.

23 October 1944 TNS

The North Ship
Legend

I saw three ships go sailing by,
Over the sea, the lifting sea,
And the wind rose in the morning sky,
And one was rigged for a long journey.

The first ship turned towards the west,
Over the sea, the running sea,
And by the wind was all possessed
And carried to a rich country.

The second turned towards the east,
Over the sea, the quaking sea,
And the wind hunted it like a beast
To anchor in captivity.

The third ship drove towards the north,
Over the sea, the darkening sea,
But no breath of wind came forth,
And the decks shone frostily.

The northern sky rose high and black
Over the proud unfruitful sea,
East and west the ships came back
Happily or unhappily:

But the third went wide and far
Into an unforgiving sea
Under a fire-spilling star,
And it was rigged for a long journey.

8 October 1944 TNS

Songs
65° N

My sleep is made cold
By a recurrent dream
Where all things seem
Sickeningly to poise
On emptiness, on stars
Drifting under the world.

When waves fling loudly
And fall at the stern,
I am wakened each dawn
Increasingly to fear
Sail-stiffening air,
The birdless sea.

Light strikes from the ice:
Like one who near death
Savours the serene breath,
I grow afraid,
Now the bargain is made,
That dream draws close.

27 October 1944 TNS

Fortunetelling

'You will go a long journey,
In a strange bed take rest,
And a dark girl will kiss you
As softly as the breast
Of an evening bird comes down
Covering its own nest.

'She will cover your mouth
Lest memory exclaim
At her bending face,
Knowing it is the same
As one who long since died
Under a different name.'

2 *November 1944* TNS

75° N
Blizzard

Suddenly clouds of snow
Begin assaulting the air,
As falling, as tangled
As a girl's thick hair.

Some see a flock of swans,
Some a fleet of ships
Or a spread winding-sheet,
But the snow touches my lips

And beyond all doubt I know
A girl is standing there
Who will take no lovers
Till she winds me in her hair.

29 October 1944 TNS

Above 80° N

'A woman has ten claws,'
Sang the drunken boatswain;
Farther than Betelgeuse,
More brilliant than Orion
Or the planets Venus and Mars,
The star flames on the ocean;
'A woman has ten claws,'
Sang the drunken boatswain.

31 October 1944 TNS

'Coming at last to night's most thankful springs'

Coming at last to night's most thankful springs,
I meet a runner's image, sharply kept
Ambered in memory from mythology;
A man who never turned aside and slept,
Nor put on masks of love; to whom all things
Were shadowlike against the news he bore,
Pale as the sky: one who for certainty
Had not my hesitations, lest he see
The loud and precious scroll of sounding shields
Not worth the carrying, when held before
The full moon travelling through her shepherdless fields.

1 March 1945 ITGOL

Plymouth

A box of teak, a box of sandalwood,
A brass-ringed spyglass in a case,
A coin, leaf-thin with many polishings,
Last kingdom of a gold forgotten face,
These lie about the room, and daily shine
When new-built ships set out towards the sun.

If they had any roughness, any flaw,
An unfamiliar scent, all this has gone;
They are no more than ornaments, or eyes,
No longer knowing what they looked upon,
Turned sightless; rivers of Eden, rivers of blood
Once blinded them, and were not understood.

The hands that chose them rust upon a stick.
Let my hands find such symbols, that can be
Unnoticed in the casual light of day,
Lying in wait for half a century
To split chance lives across, that had not dreamed
Such coasts had echoed, or such seabirds screamed.

25 June 1945 Mandrake, May 1946, ITGOL

'Lift through the breaking day'

Lift through the breaking day,
  Wind that pursues the dawn:
Under night's heedless stone
Houses and river lay –
  Now to the east they shine.

Climb the long summer hills
  Where the wide trees are spread,
Drown the cold-shadowed wood
With noise of waterfalls;
  And under chains of cloud

Fly on towards the sea:
  Sing there upon the beach
Till all's beyond death's reach,
And empty shells reply
  That all things flourish.

27 August 1945 ITGOL

Portrait

Her hands intend no harm:
Her hands devote themselves
To sheltering a flame;
Winds are her enemies,
And everything that strives
To bring her cold and darkness.

But wax and wick grow short:
These she so dearly guards
Despite her care die out;
Her hands are not strong enough
Her hands will fall to her sides
And no wind will trouble to break her grief.

7 November 1945 Mandrake, May 1946, ITGOL
(as 'The quiet one')

'Past days of gales'

Past days of gales
When skies are colourless
The acorn falls,
Dies; so for this space
Autumn is motionless.

Because the sun
So hesitates in this decay,
I think we still could turn,
Speak to each other in a different way;
For ways of speaking die,

And yet the sun pardons our voices still,
And berries in the hedge
Through all the nights of rain have come to the full,
And death seems like long hills, a range
We ride each day towards, and never reach.

17 November 1945 ITGOL

'Who whistled for the wind, that it should break'

Who whistled for the wind, that it should break
Gently, on this air?
On what ground was it gathered, where
For the carrying, for its own sake,
Is night so gifted?

                        Mind never met
Image of death like this, and yet
(All winds crying for that unbroken field,
Day having lifted)
Black flowers burst out wherever the night has knelt.

15 December 1945 ITGOL

APPENDIX

Order of poems in the individual collections

The North Ship
(July 1945)

All catches alight
This was your place of birth
The moon is full tonight
Dawn
Conscript
Kick up the fire
The horns of the morning
Winter
Climbing the hill within the deafening wind
Within the dream you said
Night-Music
Like the train's beat
I put my mouth
Nursery Tale
The Dancer
The bottle is drunk out by one
To write one song, I said
If grief could burn out
Ugly Sister
I see a girl dragged by the wrists
I dreamed of an out-thrust arm of land
One man walking a deserted platform
If hands could free you, heart
Love, we must part now: do not let it be
Morning has spread again
This is the first thing
Heaviest of flowers, the head
Is it for now or for always
Pour away that youth
So through that unripe day you bore your head
The North Ship
Waiting for breakfast (*added to the first Faber edition, September 1966*)

XX Poems
(April 1951)

Wedding-wind: 'The wind blew all my wedding-day'
Modesties: 'Words as plain as hen-birds' wings'
'Always too eager for the future, we'
'Even so distant, I can taste the grief'
'Latest face, so effortless'
Arrival: 'Morning, a glass door, flashes'
'Since the majority of me'
Spring: 'Green-shadowed people sit, or walk in rings'
'Waiting for breakfast, while she brushed her hair'
Two portraits of sex. I Oils: 'Sun. Tree. Beginning. God in a thicket.
  Crown'
II Etching: 'Endlessly, time-honoured irritant'
'On longer evenings'
'Since we agreed to let the road between us'
'If my darling were once to decide'
'Who called love conquering'
'The widest prairies have electric fences'
The dedicated: 'Some must employ the scythe'
Wants: 'Beyond all this, the wish to be alone'
'There is an evening coming in'
At grass: 'The eye can hardly pick them out'

The Fantasy Poets No. 21
(March 1954)

Lines on a Young Lady's Photograph Album: 'At last you yielded up
  the album, which'
Whatever Happened?: 'At once whatever happened starts receding'
If, My Darling: 'If my darling were once to decide'
Arrivals, Departures: 'This town has docks where channel boats come
  sidling'
At Grass: 'The eye can hardly pick them out'

The Less Deceived
(The Marvell Press, November 1955)

[315]

The Whitsun Weddings
(February 1964)

High Windows
(June 1974)

Unpublished typescript: *In the Grip of Light*
(1947)

The quiet one: 'Her hands intend no harm'
Getaway: 'One man walking a deserted platform'
'Many famous feet have trod'
Night-Music: 'At one the wind rose'
To a Very Slow Air: 'The golden sheep are feeding, and'
Träumerei: 'In this dream that dogs me I am part'
'Within the dream, you said'
'Some must employ the scythe'
Winter: 'In the field, two horses'
Deep Analysis: 'I am a woman lying on a leaf'
Thaw: 'Tiny immortal streams are on the move'
Dying day: 'There is an evening coming in'
Two Guitar Pieces: I 'The tin-roofed shack by the railroad'
                       II 'I roll a cigarette, and light'
'And the wave sings because it is moving'

Notes

'Poem about Oxford' was written on the flyleaf of *An Oxford University Chest* by John Betjeman: 1970 edition, S. R. Publishers Ltd.

'The little lives of earth and form' was written on the flyleaf of *Thorburn's Mammals* with an introduction by David Attenborough: Ebury Press & Michael Joseph, 1974; in longhand, inscribed 'To Monica with all love from Philip 1977'. (Alexander Thorburn, 1860–1935, 'now recognized as an outstanding illustrator of animals and birds of Western Europe': originally published as *British Mammals*, 2 vols, 1920–1.)

'In times when nothing stood' was commissioned by the Trustees of Queen Square Garden for the Silver Jubilee in 1977. It is incised in stone, along with a poem by Ted Hughes, in Queen Square, London, and was reproduced by the National Hospital (also in Queen Square) on its 1978 Christmas card.

'New eyes each year' was the fiftieth-anniversary keepsake for the Brynmor Jones Library, Hull, and was printed on an Imperial Albion press there in March 1979.

'The daily things we do' was written for Brenda Moon, Larkin's deputy at the University Library in Hull for twelve years, on the occasion of the fiftieth anniversary of the library's opening. Larkin wrote it alongside the 'public' poem composed for the same occasion ('New eyes each year') and left it on her desk as a surprise. Brenda Moon is now Librarian of Edinburgh University.

'Good for you, Gavin' was written for Gavin Ewart's sixty-fifth birthday in 1981 at the request of Margo Ewart.

'Long lion days' was written on 21 July 1982 in longhand on a small single sheet tucked into Notebook 8, which otherwise ends in November 1980.

'By day, a lifted study-storehouse' was an eightieth-birthday greeting to Sir Brynmor Jones from the Library Committee and the staff of the Brynmor Jones Library, University of Hull, in October 1983 and was printed on an Imperial Albion press at the university.

'Last Will and Testament' was the joint work of Larkin and B. N. Hughes (b.1921), who was at King Henry VIII School, Coventry. Noel Hughes went up to St John's College, Oxford, with Larkin in October 1940.

Index of titles

Index of first lines

Is it for now or for always, 296
Isolate city spread alongside water, 203
It's easy to write when you've nothing to write about, 216

Jake Balokowsky, my biographer, 170
Jan van Hogspeuw staggers to the door, 177

Kick up the fire, and let the flames break loose, 285

Lambs that learn to walk in snow, 112
Latest face, so effortless, 53
Lift through the breaking day, 308
Light spreads darkly downwards from the high, 163
Like the train's beat, 288
Lonely in Ireland, since it was not home, 104
Long lion days, 219
Long roots moor summer to our side of earth., 96
Love again: wanking at ten past three, 215
Love, we must part now: do not let it be, 280

Mantled in grey, the dusk steals slowly in, 225
Many famous feet have trod, 15
Marrying left your maiden name disused., 101
Morning, a glass door, flashes, 51
Morning at last: there in the snow, 206
Morning has spread again, 281
Most people know more as they get older, 211
My age fallen away like white swaddling, 95
My dear Kafka, 38
My mother, who hates thunderstorms, 68
My sleep is made cold, 302
My wife and I have asked a crowd of craps, 181

Never to walk from the station's lamps and laurels, 79
New eyes each year, 212
Next year we are to bring the soldiers home, 171
No, I have never found, 99
None of the books have time, 124
No one gives you a thought, as day by day, 22
Nothing significant was really said, 235
Now night perfumes lie upon the air, 227

Obedient daily dress, 92
Oh, no one can deny, 117
On longer evenings, 33
On pillow after pillow lies, 194
On shallow slates the pigeons shift together, 109
On shallow straw, in shadeless glass, 130
On short, still days, 91
On the day of the explosion, 175
Once I am sure there's nothing going on, 97
Once I believed in you, 46